FOR YOUNG CHAMPIONS

by Robert J. Antonacci and Gene Schoor

illustrated by Frank Mullins

McGRAW-HILL BOOK COMPANY

New York   St. Louis   San Francisco   Düsseldorf   Johannesburg
Kuala Lumpur   London   Mexico   Montreal   New Delhi
Panama   Rio de Janeiro   Singapore   Sydney   Toronto

Also by Robert J. Antonacci (and Jene Barr)
BASEBALL FOR YOUNG CHAMPIONS
FOOTBALL FOR YOUNG CHAMPIONS
BASKETBALL FOR YOUNG CHAMPIONS
PHYSICAL FITNESS FOR YOUNG CHAMPIONS

Robert J. Antonacci is the coauthor of
SPORTS OFFICIATING

Also by Gene Schoor
YOUNG ROBERT KENNEDY

Library of Congress Cataloging in Publication Data

Antonacci, Robert Joseph, date
  Track and field for young champions.

  SUMMARY: Examines the history, equipment, rules,
and techniques of each event in track and field.
  1. Track-athletics—Juvenile literature. [1. Track
and field] I. Schoor, Gene, joint author.
II. Mullins, Frank, illus. III. Title.
GV1060.5.A57 1974   796.4′2   73–17761
ISBN 0–07–002135–X
ISBN 0–07–002136–8 (lib. bdg.)

123456789 BPBP 7987654

Contents

1

Track and Field
—A World Sport

"The Champions Are Off!"

The sharp report of the starter's gun rings out. The race is on. Look at Terry, number six, sprint ahead as he flashes by the front of the pack.

All the runners are moving swiftly and close together on the specially designed running track. Now Terry is in the lead, with Jerry coming up fast and closing in on Terry in the back stretch.

The fans in the huge stadium are yelling. Can number six hold the lead? Number three, Jerry, is trailing, but gaining.

Suddenly, like a jet engine picking up speed to cross the sound barrier, Terry uncorks a tremendous burst of speed and bursts across the finish line—the winner in a new World and Olympic sprint record time.

SOARING OVER THE BAR. Across the field another group watches Bobby getting set for the high jump inside the beautiful oval track. The crossbar is approaching a record height.

Bobby is leaning slightly forward, his eyes fixed on the crossbar. His entire body is tensed for the task ahead. Slowly he lifts his head, looks at the crossbar once again, and starts to run. The crowd is silent. Bobby picks up speed as he reaches the bar. With perfect timing he springs high into the air and sends his body soaring over the crossbar.

These are examples of only two well-trained athletes. This is modern-day championship competition. Did you know that in practically every country in the world you can see boys and girls, men and women taking part in some form of running, jumping, and throwing contests?

It certainly was different many ages ago. For many centuries man had to know how to run, jump, and throw well in order to survive and protect himself and his family

MYRON'S DISKIBOLOS
Bronze Statue of a Greek athlete 2500 years ago

from other tribes and wild beasts. During the Greek period of history skills became important in the training of great warriors. It was during this period of history that early athletic contests began.

Early Greek Sports Festivals

There were constant wars among the different tribes in ancient Greece. The land was seldom at peace. Quarrels between neighboring city-states were frequent. At a moment's notice, small wars would start. The safety of the people depended upon the warriors' physical fitness.

VICTORY SPORTS FESTIVALS. After a war was won, a tribe would celebrate the victory by holding a sports festival. The leading athletes, who were also the greatest warriors, competed for the championships of their tribe in foot racing, jumping, and in throwing the discus and javelin. Chariot racing, wrestling, and boxing were also part of the competition.

FUNERAL GAMES. Many of the small states would hold special athletic contests called "funeral games" to honor the death of a popular warrior.

SPORTS-HERO FESTIVALS. These sports festivals were given only in honor of the great gods or sports heroes. Two of these gods were Apollo and Hercules.

Sports were an important part of the daily life of the Greeks, and sports heroes were honored as special members of each tribe. The tribes loved competition in everyday life, and in due course the competition in sports was to become the most important event in the life of the Greek people.

Now let us see how champions from every country were to have a chance to compete for the world championships.

The wisest men in ancient Greece had a wonderful idea—one that would stop the constant wars between tribes. They suggested that the rulers and chieftains of every tribe send their champions to compete in one mighty festival to determine the championship of all Greece. Skills in running, jumping, and throwing were to be especially prominent.

So, over 2,500 years ago, the leaders of every tribe halted their conflicts long enough to have the champions take part in the *first Olympic games*. The games were held on the plain of Olympia in Greece in 776 B.C. They were so successful that specific rules were drafted, and the leaders agreed to hold the Olympic games every four years.

FIRST OLYMPIC-GAME RULES. The rules that were to govern these early games were written on a discus (*diskos*), a round flat stone. Competition to throw the discus developed among the strongest men. The discus champion was known as the greatest athlete in the land and was honored and feted by the entire nation. He was the hero of heroes.

ROMAN RULERS END OLYMPICS. After the Romans conquered Greece, the Olympic games began to cause arguments between the Greek and Roman Empires. Some athletes were competing as professionals instead of as amateurs. The winners now sought money and gifts instead of the simple olive branch. So, after 1,100 years of Ancient Olympic competition, Emperor Theodosius I of Rome halted all future games. The Olympic temples were destroyed by barbarian invaders and the Olympic stadium was destroyed.

For 1,500 years there was no competition to decide who were the world track and field champions. Then England and other nations began to organize their own tournaments.

The first public school to promote track and field competition was Eton in England in 1837. The first time two different university teams met in track and field events occurred in England in 1864 between Oxford and Cambridge, and the competition reactivated great interest in track and field meets. In 1866 the British Isles Championships were held. The meet was so interesting and successful that there was a great clamor for the revival of the Olympic games. Thirty years later, in 1896, the first modern Olympic games were held in Greece.

Modern Olympic Games

The amateur spirit, excitement, and competition attracted the attention of Baron Pierre de Coubertin of France. Baron de Coubertin was born in Paris in January, 1863, and his family mapped out a military career for him. He attended the famous French military school at St. Cyr. He studied political science, education, and international problems. He visited schools and colleges in Europe and in the United States.

Since young people and sports have gone together from the dawn of human history, Baron de Coubertin decided that education and athletics together could develop a new and better understanding among nations. The Baron persuaded many men in many countries to aid him in reawakening the Olympic spirit and the games. After great effort he succeeded, and the first Modern Olympic games were held at Athens, Greece, in 1896.

TRACK AND FIELD PROGRAM. There were six track and six field events in this first Modern Olympics. Only ten Americans were entered, all in the track events. But when it came time to compete in the field events, a few of the Americans entered anyway. And they actually won nine out of twelve Olympic championships in both the track and the field events!

FIRST MODERN OLYMPIC CHAMPION. James Connolly of the United States won the first Olympic championship event. It was in the "hop-hop-jump," which is known today as the "hop-step-jump." He had never before competed in this event until the day he arrived in Athens for the competition.

Track and Field in America

What people first competed in track events in America? Indians!

INDIANS—THE FOOT RACERS. The Indians were competing in foot racing and spear throwing hundreds of years before Columbus landed in America. They often ran over a thirty-mile course just for endurance training. Spear throwing was another skill they practiced. They competed in these events as young warriors. They also competed in these events during religious games, and in addition used them to determine the champions of the tribe.

TRACK IN COLONIAL PERIOD. There are records showing that most youngsters in Colonial America organized their own games of running, jumping, and throwing. But the real competition at this time was among adults only. Foot races for prizes are recorded as early as 1680 in Massachusetts and 1691 in Virginia. Wherever the early settlers gathered for corn-husking bees or town sports, foot racing and feats of throwing were always part of the competition.

GEORGE WASHINGTON—THE JAVELIN THROWER? In 1772, when Washington was forty years old, some young friends were visiting him at his home in Mount Vernon. Colonel Washington saw that several of them were competing in an event called "pitching the bar." That was a popular sport in those days. The bar was made of iron and weighed several pounds. Washington asked his friends if they would show him the peg that marked the farthest pitch. Then Washington took the iron bar in his hand, stepped to the line, and with a tremendous thrust of his arm, hurled the missile into the air. The bar sailed through the air, landing farther than the record throw. Colonel Washington turned to his young friends and said, "When you beat my pitch, let me know." They never beat his throw.

Do you think President Washington could have been a champion javelin thrower today?

ANDREW JACKSON. Jackson, who was president from 1829 to 1837, might have been a champion shot-putter. He was known to be a champion at "throwing the long bullet." This was a sport where you would throw or, as sportsmen say, "put" a six-pound iron ball at a certain marked goal.

PROFESSIONAL RUNNERS. In the 1800's, the foot races were mainly run by professionals. People would wager on their favorite "pedestrians"—or "peds"—as the runners were called at that time.

Races were first run through the city streets with men on horseback clearing the way. Large crowds lined the route of the runners.

The races soon became so popular that the promoters held the events on "racecourses" where the spectators were charged admission. These racecourses were not yet

7

as developed as the modern track and field facilities of to-day.

As many as 30,000 people went to see a popular race in New York in 1835. The promoter—the man who arranged the races—offered $1,000 to any man who could run a ten-mile course in under an hour.

Champion runners would challenge runners from other cities and also challenge runners from England.

PROFESSIONAL WALKERS. International walking races were very popular during the same period. American champions would challenge walkers from England and Ireland. Most of the races were for long distances. One race in 1867 involved a walk from Portland, Maine, to Chicago, Illinois, in twenty-six days and the winner received a $10,000 prize.

One event that influenced indoor track as we know it today took place at Gilmore's Garden, later known as Madison Square Garden, in New York. This event, held in 1878, was a six-day walking championship race.

FIRST CINDER TRACK. For hundreds of years athletes ran on all kinds of terrain. There were no special running tracks.

The New York Athletic Club, founded in 1868, began sponsoring many track and field meets. In 1871, they built what was to be the first outdoor cinder track, and invited runners, both amateur and professional to compete in the first track meet in the United States.

Today the tracks are made of boards, rubberized asphalt, cinders, grass-tex, fine crushed brick, and clay. The modern tracks are designed and built by experts who specialize in this work. All-weather tracks are best.

TRACK AND FIELD ORGANIZATIONS. The sport of track and field, as we know it today, began to spread into the colleges after the Civil War period. In 1874, the *first inter-*

collegiate track meet was held at Saratoga, New York.

The *Intercollegiate Association of Amateur Athletics of America* (representing the Eastern colleges) and the *National Collegiate Athletic Association* (representing colleges from all over the country) were founded in 1876. Today a meet is sponsored every year to decide who the National Collegiate Athletic Association (NCAA) champion is for every track and field event.

In 1888, the *Amateur Athletic Union* (AAU) was organized. This group sponsors a meet every year. Today the winners often compete against track and field champions from countries throughout the world.

The first International Amateur Track and Field Meet took place in 1895 at Manhattan Field, New York, between the New York Athletic Club and the London Athletic Club.

Competition began to spread into the high schools so rapidly after World War I that school officials asked for an organization that would control and regulate high-school athletics. In 1922, the *National Federation of State High School Athletic Associations* was formed. All of the organizations named keep accurate records to determine who their champions are.

Keeper of World's Records

Just about every country in the world has competition in track and field. The *International Amateur Athletic Federation* (IAAF) was formed in 1913 to set up rules for all worldwide track and field competitions. Practically every country, large or small, is a member of this federation today. Before this organization approves a record, it will study the conditions under which the meet was held.

FIRST STARTER'S GUN. During the early Greek games, a runner would receive severe punishment if he made an unfair start in a race. But as late as the nineteenth century, many different methods were used to start a race. Before a race, the competitors would agree on the method to be used. Many runners try to trick opponents with an earlier start.

Before the end of the nineteenth century, however, meet officials agreed to use a "starter's pistol."

FIRST TIMER'S WATCHES. Instruments to measure the speed of an athlete in a race were in use during the first half of the nineteenth century. They were not very accurate, however. Adolphe Nicole of Switzerland invented the first *chronograph*. The chronograph is an instrument for measuring and recording intervals of time.

Modern stopwatches used for timing track events are the highest-quality instruments. They record speed to one-tenth ($\frac{1}{10}$) of one second. An instrument called the *chronoscope* is available to record speed time to one-hundredth ($\frac{1}{100}$) of a second.

Uniforms

In ancient Greece, track men wore only a loincloth. They wore no shoes or shirt. One day the loincloth fell off a runner during a race. He won the race so easily that for many years the men ran naked. This was accepted as appropriate in ancient Greece.

In early America, there was no special clothing for foot racing. The professional pedestrian runners of 1840–60 wore colorful clothes of their own choosing. One runner wore a green shirt, blue breeches, white stockings, red belt, and red shoes tipped with blue.

After the Civil War period, men began to wear special track and field clothing: shorts that reached to the knees and shirts of many different colors.

THE FIRST SPIKED TRACK SHOES. The first spiked track shoes began to appear on the scene after 1868, when an

American amateur sprinter, William Curtis, wore spiked shoes and won many races. Today there are several choices of shoes to be worn for the different track and field events.

WOMEN'S SPECIAL UNIFORMS. These began to appear much later. Women ran mostly in their regular everyday dress. Vassar College for girls is given credit for adopting, in 1866, a special uniform that was later used for many

STATUE OF GIRL RUNNER
2500 YEARS AGO IN GREECE

sports. One-piece black suits appeared in 1900, and the "middy and bloomers" in 1910. Later, the popular knickers-and-blouse uniforms became universally accepted.

Girls' track and field uniforms, today, are similar to those of the boys.

More Track and Field History

Championship track and field records are broken every year. This is not an accident. Manufacturers develop better equipment and faster tracks. Doctors help coaches with improved diet and training methods. Here are some additional historical developments that have helped to make track and field the popular sport it is today.

THE EARLY SPRINT STARTS. For many centuries athletes began a sprint race from a standing position. In 1884, a popular Scottish champion won many races from a "crouched start." Most runners adopted this method in the belief that it would give them a fast start. Several years later, a Yale University sprinter was the first to take a starting position "on all fours." He won many races using this start, and soon every sprinter began to use this position for a quick getaway at the "go" signal. Runners also began to "dig" little holes on the track to place their toes behind the starting line.

More improvements and more records were broken with another invention. This was the invention, in 1927, by two doctors at the University of Iowa, of the "starting blocks." The blocks of wood were "spiked" into the ground, giving the runner confidence when pushing off against them for a speedy start.

THE FIRST TRACK HURDLES. The earliest hurdle races held under specific rules were said to have taken place in a meet held at Eton, England, about 1850. The first hurdles (sometimes called barriers) were made of "solid sheep hurdles," three feet, six inches high and rigidly staked into a meadow or field.

About the year 1880, the Americans used hurdles that stretched all the way across the track. A large stake at each side of the track held up a crossbar. If one runner knocked the crossbar down, it was down for all runners. In 1900, a movable and single hurdle in the shape of a *T* was staked to the ground.

Today each runner sails over his own hurdles.

Boys' and Girls' Championships

Did you know that track and field meets for young people are very popular in the United States? Elementary schools have developed special rules for young boys and girls who wish to take part in track and field events. City recreation departments, YMCA, Boys Clubs, CYO, Boy Scouts, Girl Scouts, and neighborhood clubs also sponsor meets for youngsters.

Later on in this book you will learn more about the different events that youngsters can participate in for championships. You will also learn how to train and improve in each of the events.

2

Getting to Know
Track and Field

One of the best places to enjoy a sunny day is at a track and field meet. There you will discover a great number of athletes scattered around the stadium. Some are pacing themselves on the beautiful running track. Other athletes are practicing jumping and throwing skills inside the oval track area. Many more are working on "warm-up" exercises. Soon you will become aware that the sport of championship track and field, like a circus, is made up of many different events. The number and kinds of events depend on the type of competition. Is it an Olympic, college, school, or a young boys and girls club meet?

You can become a champion in one skill, or a champion in more than one. A track and field meet has an event that is suitable and interesting for each boy and girl. Knowing more about this worldwide sport will increase your enjoyment of what is taking place on the field of competition. It will also help you to decide which events are the most challenging for you.

Before the Meet

Read your newspapers. Watch track and field meets on TV. Try to see your favorite local team in action.

Newspapers will give the names of the athletes, their

home towns, their schools, events they have entered, and their best records. At the meets, you can get a program in which you will find the listings of the athletes' numbers, their heights, weights, and ages.

The Sports Stadium

As you enter the stadium you will see the *running track,* which is a strip of level ground used for foot racing. It is oval-shaped and is usually constructed around a football or soccer field. Indoor tracks are usually of one-eighth (⅛) mile distance; outdoor tracks of one-quarter (¼) mile distance. The width of the track depends on the amount of space available and determines whether four or as many as eight sprinters start in a race at one time.

The track is painted with lines called running lanes. Each runner in the dash and sprint races must run in his own assigned lane from the beginning to the end of the race.

Foot races and hurdle races are held on a track. All the athletes run with their left sides facing the inside of the track. This is known as running *counterclockwise.*

THE FIELD. The space inside the oval track is known as the *Field Event Area.* Some of these events are the shot-put, the running long jump, and the high jump. Athletes even compete in baseball and basketball throws for distance.

For reasons of safety many of the field events, such as the discus and javelin throws, are often held on an entirely different field than the one where track competition is being held.

Different Kinds of Meets

A track and field meet usually lasts from one to three hours. The time depends on the kind of meet being held.

A competition between two track and field teams is called a *Dual Meet*. A *Triangular Meet* involves competition among three teams, and a *Quadrangular Meet* involves four teams. A *Multiple Meet* involves more than four teams.

Conference Meets are between teams or individuals belonging to a certain league or conference. *National Championship Meets* are very large meets and may take one to three full days. They include teams and individuals competing from all parts of the country. And, of course, the *Olympic Games* are very large meets involving teams and individuals from all over the world. These games may last for many days.

A track and field games committee decides how the time schedule of events shall take place. They also decide on the number of events each contestant may enter in one meet. Most athletes are not allowed to compete in more than four events in a meet.

Doctor's Examination

Before an athlete is accepted for competition in a championship track and field event, he must show that he was approved by a doctor. This physical examination assures the meet officials that the athlete is healthy and properly conditioned for the competition.

Practice before Regular Competition

Did you know that coaches insist that all competitors have a definite number of practice days before they enter a championship meet?

Junior high school athletes are asked to complete at least fifteen practice sessions before participating in a real meet.

Athletes in grades below junior high should practice until a doctor or physical education teacher approves their readiness for participation.

WHAT IS A HEAT? A *heat* is a preliminary race to determine which runners will *qualify* for the final race. Heats are held in meets only when more sprinters are entered than there are lanes available for a race.

For example: If you have eighteen runners entered for the 100-yard dash and the track provides only six lanes, only six sprinters can run at a time. So there will be three heats, and the first two winners of each heat will run in the finals to determine the champion.

Warm-up Practice

Look at the competitors on the field just before they take part in the actual contest! What do you see? The athlete entered in the hurdles event is lifting his foot up on a hurdle to stretch his leg muscles. Sprinters are practicing quick starts. A shot-putter is practicing his steps in the shot-put circle. Everyone is getting ready with last-minute loosening-up exercises before going all out in the real competition.

False-start Rule

At the beginning of a race the official starter gives all runners instructions. With the call of *"on your marks,"* the runners immediately take their starting positions. The official then commands the runners to *"get set."* No runner is allowed to touch or lean over the starting line with any part of the body. The runners then remain in the "set" position, motionless for two seconds. Now, the starter fires his pistol to give the *"go"* signal.

If a runner leaves his mark before the pistol is fired, or if he moves after the "set" instructions, it is called a "false start." The runner receives a warning. Two "false starts" and the runner is disqualified.

Photo-finish Rule

The finish line for a foot race is drawn on the ground across the track. To help officials decide the winner of a close race, a soft piece of yarn is stretched across the track directly above the finish line. The yarn is attached four feet above the ground to posts located on each side of the track.

The runner whose "torso" (chest region) breaks the yarn or tape and crosses the line first is declared the winner. Each runner whose torso crosses the line after the winner places second, third, and so on to the last.

If a runner breaks the yarn with his hand or head, it does not count.

Passing a Runner—Going for Pole Lane

The *Pole Lane* is usually called "lane one" on the track. It is the lane on the inside portion of the track. In long-distance races and in races where a runner is allowed to cross the path of another runner, you will notice that the competitors try to gain the pole-lane position.

A runner must be at least one normal running stride past another runner before he can cross his path. The normal running stride measures about seven feet for school and college meets. A runner who "bumps" or accidentally "pushes" another competitor when trying to pass or to cross his path is disqualified from the race.

Staggered Start

A specific starting line is painted on each lane of the track. In the relays or sprints, each runner must stay in his own lane from beginning to end. The runners in the outer lanes start the race a marked distance ahead of the runners in the lanes closer to the pole lane. The pole lane around a complete oval-curve track is shorter in length than all other lanes. The outside lane is the longest in length, therefore the runner in this lane gets the biggest headstart over the other runners. Each runner, however, covers the same distance to the finish line. The runner in the second lane starts running from a position a certain distance ahead of the pole-lane runner, the third-lane runner starts a certain distance ahead of the second-lane runner, the fourth-lane runner ahead of the third-lane runner, and so on.

Field Event Trials

In the trials for the *pole vault* and *high jump* each competitor is allowed *three trials* to make a successful jump or vault over any one height.

Each competitor in the running long jump, the hop-step-jump, and in the discus, shot-put, and javelin events is allowed *four preliminary trials*. Preliminary trials are held only when a large number of contestants are entered in a meet. Those contestants qualifying for the final competition are allowed *three more trials*.

The best performance (jump or throw) by a competitor, regardless of whether it occurs in the preliminary trials or in the final trials, is declared the winning one.

Scoring

When two teams meet in a track and field competition, the contestant earns *five points for first place, three points for second place,* and *one point for third place.* After adding the points scored by each competitor on each team, the team with the most points wins the meet.

In large championship meets, where many teams are entered, the scoring is much different. The winner is often given *ten points for first place* and even a competitor coming in *sixth place* is given *one point.*

More information on scoring for all events can be found in a later chapter in this book.

Now that you have some idea of what championship track and field is about, let's start in and learn the different skills needed to become a participant.

3

Get that Speed

(How to Sprint)

"Race you to the corner." "Tag." "Hide and seek." "Beat you to the tree." These are examples of games and contests boys and girls use to show their speed.

First Event in Ancient Olympics

The very first event in the Ancient Olympic Games was a foot race to measure man's speed. The race was called a "staid" or "stadium race," because the distance was one length of the stadium—about 210 yards.

Early runners ran barefoot. The running track was mainly filled with sand. Start and finish lines were marked with stone threshholds or slabs of smooth marble.

Sprint Racing Today

Sprint races today are held on specially designed indoor and outdoor tracks. They are races of short distances and are also known as *"dashes."*

Until your body grows bigger and stronger, you should spend your time *only* on the shorter sprint races. Learn and practice the skills needed to run short dashes. This is the way the champions started.

Speed distances for outdoor championships go from 100-yard, 220-yard, to 300-yard events. The 440-yard event (one-quarter mile) is often called a sprint race.

The distances for the indoor meets usually are the forty-yard, fifty-yard, sixty-yard, and seventy-five-yard dash events.

The sprinting distance for school meets usually depends on the school grade and age of the runners.

WHY LEARN SPEED RUNNING? A jet airplane or space rocket has an engine and fuel to give it power for speed. Your body and especially your legs have muscles that can give you more speed when needed. Regardless of your height and weight, *you can improve your speed*. Even if your improvement is only one step faster than before, it will help you enjoy the many everyday sports and games much better. Also, it will help you get from one place to another faster, whether you are at home, school, or on vacation.

You need speed for making quick takeoffs, for short sprints, for running bases, going after hard-hit balls, catching and carrying a football, or breaking free for a basketball pass.

Learning to sprint faster will help improve your heart, lungs, and leg muscles and make you healthier and stronger.

Requirements of a Speed Runner

Here are some valuable pointers you must learn before you are ready to take part in the sprints. Study and remember what you read. Write these tips down in your track notebook.

(1) If you can, choose lightweight shoes with soles that will keep you from slipping when running hard.

(2) Learn how to use starting blocks or the holes dug in the surface of the track in which you place your toes for a quick start.

(3) Know the proper position of the feet, back, head, hands just before the takeoff.

(4) Get into the habit of listening for the sound of the starter's pistol "shot" or word "go."

(5) Know how long your first and second strides (steps) should be after the signal "go."

(6) Know the *leaning position* of the body soon after leaving the starting blocks.

(7) Use the correct arm action when speed running.

(8) Know how to force your feet on the track to get the explosive forward speed.

(9) Know how to make strides or steps that are low to the ground for speed running.

(10) Know how to increase the distance of your strides to help increase your speed.

(11) Know correct breathing when speed running.

(12) Know the correct form when crossing the finish line or tape.

Does this look like a lot to learn? Champions learn even more. Many of the greatest champions started at your age. Work and practice one skill at a time for now. Don't ever get discouraged. You will soon surprise yourself. Before you know it, you will begin to run faster than before!

Different Starting Positions

Did you know that there is no "best position" to start a race? All sprinters have a favorite style or stance for starting. After much practice they discover the one that is most comfortable for them.

Most sprinters will select one of the three famous starting positions. They are known as the *elongated start, bunch start,* and *medium start.*

THE ELONGATED START POSITION. After the signal "take your mark," the runner places one foot about eighteen inches behind the starting line. The knee of the

1. Bunch Start

2. Medium Start

3. Elongated Start

THREE DIFFERENT STARTING STANCES FROM "GET-SET" POSITION

other leg is placed in back, just about even with the heel of the foot in front.

In other words, an *elongated position* really means a longer length or distance between the front and rear feet. There is, also, a longer distance between the front foot and the starting line.

THE BUNCH START POSITION. In this position the distance between the rear and front feet is shorter. The rear and front feet are "bunched" closer together. The bunch start also means that the front foot is placed closer to the starting line.

THE MEDIUM START POSITION. This means that the distance between the front foot and the back foot, and the distance from starting line and front foot are somewhere in between the distances used for the bunch and elongated starting positions.

The medium start is the most popular for young runners, boys and girls, and for many champions, too. *This is the one you must practice.* When you grow older, you will try the other positions—with the help of your coach.

The "Explosive"—Medium Sprint Start

The medium start position is a great favorite with runners. Here is what you do for practice.

How do you kick a football? If you kick with your right foot, your left foot remains on the turf, giving you strength, balance, and thrust. It is the more powerful leg. In track your left foot is known as the front or *power* (*lead*) *foot* for a sprint starting position. The reason is the same. The left foot or front foot is stronger because it is used to push longer from the starting block.

If you kick with the left foot, place your right foot at the front block as the power foot, and the left at the rear block.

Have starting blocks set six to eight inches apart for a *medium start position*. This will help you achieve an "explosive" getaway.

Your front block is set ten to sixteen inches behind the starting line. The position of the front block depends upon your height and comfort.

The back block is set at a distance where the knee of your back leg is just about even with the toe of the front foot against the front block.

"On Your Marks"

When you hear that signal:

(1) Walk slightly in front of starting line and blocks.

(2) Shake your legs loosely several times to relax the muscles. Place the ball of the left or *power* foot with a forceful push flat against the front block. You are now leaning forward on two hands and the left knee.

(3) While resting on hands and left knee, loosen up your right leg by shaking it behind you several times. With a powerful push, place the right foot against the back block.

(4) Rest your back knee on the ground and bring your hands to the starting line.

(5) While sitting back lightly on your heels, swing your arms forward and backward from a hanging position a few times, just barely rubbing against your legs.

1. Take your mark!   2. Get Set!   3. Go! Explosive Start

4. Step One! Low Body   5. Step Two! Low Body

This tells you how wide apart your hands should be on the ground just behind the starting line.

(6) Close the fingers of each hand, place the thumbs inward and fingers outward directly behind and even with the starting line. Your hands now are about a shoulder-width apart.

(7) Straighten your elbows. Relax. Hold your head down but look ahead—and listen for the "get set" signal.

"Get Set"

About two seconds before the start of the race, you will hear the starter give the "get set" command. Here is what you do in the "get set" position:

(1) Move your weight slightly forward so it is equally distributed on both hands behind the starting line and the front foot.

(2) Lift the hips upward, slightly higher than the shoulders.

(3) Take a deep breath and hold it until the gun sounds, then breath normally.

(4) Have both knees pointing straight ahead.

(5) Elbows are straight with head low and neck relaxed. (If you raise up your head, your neck and shoulder muscles will get tense and tire easily.)

(6) Set your eyes on a spot about three to five feet in front of you.

(7) Keep this position—absolutely still—for two-seconds and concentrate on an "explosive" start.

"Go"

This is what you are waiting to hear. The sound of the starter's gun or the word "go." Then swiftly follow with this action:

(1) *Drive* the left arm forward and straight ahead very hard. Keep arm level with the ground.

(2) At the same time, *drive* your right arm back, with your hand no farther than the hip.

(3) Push against the front block with your left or lead foot with an explosive force.

(4) The right (rear) leg must come forward rapidly. Keep foot low, just barely clearing the ground.

(5) The hips follow the rest of your body forward. Don't move your hips upward before your first step. You are on your way to a fast start.

The *first step,* which is usually with the right (rear) foot, should feel natural and comfortable. Each sprinter decides what length his first step should be. Always make sure your first step is low and hard, driving forward. This first step, also, tells you if you are leaving the starting block in a straight line.

The *second step,* which is usually with the left (front) foot, must be kept close to the ground. The length of the stride (step) should not be too long nor so short that it will cause you loss of balance or forward motion.

Continue to keep your head low with eyes focused slightly up toward the other end of the track. Your chest stays level or parallel to the ground for the first few yards. As you pick up speed, your body will gradually rise to a full, natural sprinting position at about ten to fifteen yards from the starting line.

Now, keep swinging or driving the arm forward and straight ahead as the opposite leg reaches out far and low to the ground. Never swing your arms in front of your chest. Keep "pumping" in a straight line. This will prevent your head, shoulders, and hips from turning, thus causing you to lose ground.

Once you reach full sprinting speed, keep your body leaning slightly forward. Try to get a high knee action with your forward leg. Then force the foot to reach out far and fast in front of you, always landing on the front portion of the ball of that foot. This will keep you from making a high kick with the back leg.

Keep running hard. Keep driving your arms forward and back. Keep up the fast, low, long strides. Keep the body leaning a little forward. Try to relax. You can now see the finish tape (line) about fifteen yards away.

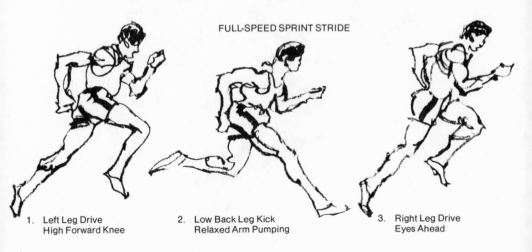

FULL-SPEED SPRINT STRIDE

1. Left Leg Drive
   High Forward Knee

2. Low Back Leg Kick
   Relaxed Arm Pumping

3. Right Leg Drive
   Eyes Ahead

When you see the *finish* tape about fifteen yards away, do not change your smooth stride and body position. Do not jump, dive, lean head back, or slow up just as you are about to hit the tape. Instead, you must recharge your body with extra fuel so you can drive through and beyond the tape with a vigorous explosive thrust—just like a rocket.

To do this thrust, pretend that you are going to run full speed ahead at least ten yards past the finish line. Remember to go through the tape with your body and shoulders leaning a little forward. Then reduce your pace to a slow trot, but continue walking until you begin to breathe normally.

This is how the champions run the dashes or sprints. With practice you can begin to look like a champion, too. Do not get discouraged if you feel that you are not improving fast enough. Take your time, and remember—practice and more practice will make you a swifter runner.

BREAKING THE TAPE AND CROSSING THE FINISH LINE

Coasting

In the longer sprint races, you may hear of a runner *coasting* for a short distance of the race. For example, this is how you use *coasting* if you are running a 150-yard dash.

1. Make a fast start and run ahead with good speed for almost fifty yards.

2. Hold the same speed (or coast) for the next fifty yards or so, but don't lose your smooth stride and sprinting form. This is the time when you are saving up energy or extra fuel for the finish.

3. Now speed up and sprint the last fifty yards, using all the extra reserve power that you didn't think you had to reach the finish tape.

In other words, coasting in the longer sprints means that you run with good speed for about one-third the distance, hold this speed (or coast) for the middle third of the race, and burst full speed, using that stored energy, for the last third of the race.

For now, you should spend time practicing the short and middle-distance sprints. Later you will work more on the 220, 330, and 440-yard dashes.

Your Speed Test

Did you know that you can take a speed test to see how you rate with other people your age throughout the country? The speed test is only one part of the total Youth Physical Fitness Test. This test was prepared by the President's Council on Physical Fitness and Sports to show how fit and active you are. The President of the United States appoints to the council people who are interested in keeping our country healthy and strong.

This test has been given to millions of boys and girls in the United States. It will help you find out if you are overweight or underweight and must watch your eating habits. Perhaps you may need to be more active in your spare time. Here is the test:

Mark a starting line and a finish line fifty yards apart.
The starter, with a timing watch in his hand, stands at the finish line.

(a) Take a sprinter's position behind the starting line.

(b) When the starter raises his hand, this is the signal to "get set."

(c) When he brings his hand down, the signal is "go!" Run as fast as you can and cross the finish line.

50-YARD DASH (BOYS)

Rating	Age— 10	11	12	13	14	15	16	17
	Time in seconds and tenths of a second							
Excellent	7.0	7.0	6.8	6.5	6.3	6.1	6.0	6.0
Presidential Award	7.4	7.4	7.0	6.9	6.6	6.4	6.2	6.1
Good	7.5	7.5	7.2	7.0	6.7	6.5	6.3	6.2
Satisfactory	8.0	7.8	7.6	7.3	7.0	6.7	6.5	6.5
Poor	8.5	8.1	8.0	7.6	7.2	7.0	6.8	6.7

Key: Running time is measured in seconds and tenths of seconds.

Example: If you are ten years old and ran the 50-yard dash in 7.4, it means seven and four-tenths seconds. If you are under ten years of age, use the test as an exercise and *do not try* to see if you can keep up with older boys and girls.

Note: Take the test without starting blocks or holes. Check your time. Then check your time with the use of starting blocks or holes.

Rating	Age— 10	11	12	13	14	15	16	17
	Time in seconds and tenths of a second							
Excellent	7.0	7.0	7.0	7.0	7.0	7.1	7.0	7.1
Presidential Award	7.5	7.6	7.5	7.5	7.4	7.5	7.5	7.5
Good	7.7	7.7	7.6	7.6	7.5	7.6	7.5	7.6
Satisfactory	8.2	8.1	8.0	8.0	7.9	8.0	8.0	8.0
Poor	8.8	8.5	8.4	8.4	8.3	8.3	8.5	8.5

Sprinting Hints

Obey health rules. Do warm-up exercises before a race.

Set the starting blocks at a distance that feels most comfortable to you.

On the signal "get set," concentrate on the race. Forget everything else.

Never look to see how another sprinter is doing. Keep your eyes focused on the finish tape.

Try moving your legs faster than your opponents'. Turn on speed. Keep your strides long and close to the ground.

Contact the ground with explosive force with each forward stride.

Always drive off hard with the rear leg.

Relax throughout the sprint. Keep the neck and shoulders feeling loose. Do not clench your fist. It tenses or tightens your muscles.

Sprinting Drills

Skip rope, do stretching and bending exercises as often as possible.

Practice "wind sprints." This is done by starting with a slow sprint for fifteen to twenty yards. Then a tremendous burst of speed for twenty-five yards. Slow down again for fifteen to twenty yards. Start all over again. Stop when you begin to tire out. This exercise develops your "wind" and lungs.

Work on quick starts with or without the use of starting blocks or holes. After the "get set" signal, keep your body still for two seconds until you hear the signal "go." Practice with a partner, each taking turns acting as a starter.

To help develop sprinter's legs, lean your body against a solid wall or tree with arms stretched about chest high. With forward, high knee action start pumping or driving your legs forward and down. Feel the muscles in your legs working?

PARTNER LEG-DRIVING DRILL. Face a partner about your own age and weight. Stretch your arms forward and place the hands on your partner's shoulders. Move legs slightly back so that you both will be leaning against each other. Now with forward high knee action start pumping and driving your legs forward and down.

Place a two-inch by four-inch board or stack of magazines on the floor. Face the board and place your toes over the edge. Now start raising your heels off the floor. Then lower them. Repeat several times.

RUNNING IN YOUR OWN LANE EXERCISE. Draw a straight line on the ground, or use baseball or football field lines already available. Try sprinting as near the straight line as possible, without turning your head or swinging your arms across your chest.

Get an old stool or hard wooden box about the height of a chair. Practice stepping on top of the stool first with your right leg, then your left leg. Bring down the right leg, then the left leg. Repeat several times.

BASEBALL. Make believe you are sprinting to first base to beat out a bunt. Sprint for a two-base hit. A three-base hit. Make believe you are stealing second base.

FOOTBALL. Get into a crouch position. Make believe you are an end sprinting twenty-five yards down field to catch a pass. Now make believe you are a defensive back. Your opponent has just barely passed you to receive a pass. With a burst of speed you turn, dash fifteen yards, jump high in the air to block the pass and prevent a touchdown.

BASKETBALL. The other team scores a basket. The referee gives you the ball outside the court. With a burst of speed you dash past your opponent toward the opposite end of the court. You are clear for a fast-break pass and an easy lay-up for the basket. This time the player you were guarding dashes away and is free for a basket. With lightning speed you sprint down the court, intercept the pass, and move down the court for another score.

SOCCER. Pretend you must run twenty yards down the field to beat your opponent for a loose soccer ball. Or make a quick start to get free for your partner's kick-pass to you and a score.

As you can see *speed* is important in many sports. Practice a little as often as possible to improve on your sprinter's skills. And don't get discouraged in your performance. Mastering just a few extra skills will cause improvement in your performance. Also you will have more fun, and be more physically fit and healthy.

4

Distance Running and Endurance Events

(Running Far and Long)

Let's test your wind and breathing. Sprint for a bus or streetcar. Do you puff and gasp for air? Do you "run out of steam" long before a game is over? Perhaps it takes you a long time to get back to normal breathing after a heavy workout? If any of these things happen to you, it could mean you need improved heart and breathing endurance.

Track Men and Staying Power

Athletes who compete in distance running or in one event after another must have superior heart and breathing endurance. They must have the *stamina* and *staying power* to last and finish the long and enduring competition. They must train for many hours to build a strong heart and lungs.

Later you will learn how you can take a running test that will rate you for heart and breathing endurance. You will, also, learn many pointers that can help you improve your stamina and staying power. Before you take in any of these athletic events, get a doctor's examination and permission from your parents and coach.

Now, let's find out what these distance running and endurance events are, where they first started, and other interesting facts.

Track events between 330 yards and 1,000 yards are usually called *middle-distance races*. Some coaches say that the one-half mile (880 yards) and the one-mile run are the only real middle-distance races.

In America the most popular middle-distance races are the 440-yard, 880-yard, and the mile. Similar events in the Olympics and International competition are called the 400-meter race, which is about 437 yards, the 800-meter race, which is about 875 yards, and 1,500-meter race, which is about 1,640 yards.

THE 440-YARD EVENT. This is usually one lap around a quarter-mile track. The event originated in the British Isles between 1850 and 1860. Later this race made its way to America. Now it is a regular event in schools and colleges. The 400-meter race became a regular Olympic event in 1896.

THE 880-YARD EVENT. Often this is called the half-mile or two-lap race around the track. This race was first run in England by professional runners about 1870. The first 880-yard race between a runner from England and America took place in 1888 at Oxford, England. The event was first held in America in New York City in 1895. The similar 800-meter race became an Olympic event in 1896. The 880-yard run is a regular event in schools and colleges in America today.

THE MILE RACE. Many track experts and fans call this race the most glamorous or popular event of a championship meet. The race covers four laps around a quarter-mile track. Some historians have recorded that one-mile races were held as early as 1822 in England. From 30,000 to 50,000 fans gathered in the old New York Polo Grounds in 1882 to see the English champions race.

Soon after this, the mile race became very popular in American schools and colleges. The 1,500-meter race, which is similar to the mile race, has been a regular Olympic event since 1896.

Long-distance Races

Many track experts feel that any foot race over one mile in length is a long-distance race. Others will say that long-distance racing begins with the one-mile event.

The most popular long-distance race in America is the two-mile event. Three-mile and six-mile races are also run, but are not as popular. The best-known races in International competition are the 5,000-meter and 10,000-meter races. These are similar to the three-mile and six-mile events.

THE TWO-MILE RACE. This popular race is sponsored by some schools and most colleges and universities.

THE 5,000-METER AND 10,000-METER RACES. These are Olympic and International competition events.

Long-distance foot-racing competition was really started in the British Isles as early as the seventeenth century and continued into the twentieth century. Most of the competitors were professional runners and walkers called "pedestrians" or "peds." There was an International ten-mile race at Hoboken, New Jersey, in 1844, in which champions from every section of the country competed before 25,000 fans for a $700 prize. Endurance running, as well as walking contests, became very popular in America and Canada.

One of the most popular long-distance runners in America and England was the Seneca Indian known as "Deerfoot." In 1860, he won many races dressed in breechcloth and moccasins, and with colored feathers in

"AMERICAN DEER" (WILLIAM JACKSON), CHAMPION PEDESTRIAN—1840

his hair. He was acclaimed throughout the United States for his championship performance and his proud bearing.

The Marathon Race

The word *marathon* means a contest of long duration, such as a twenty-inning baseball game. In track and field it means an unusually long distance run. The distance of a championship marathon race today is about twenty-six miles plus 385 yards. This race received its name and distance when a Greek messenger ran all the way from a village called Marathon to Athens in 490 B.C. to carry news that his countrymen had defeated the Persian Army in an historic battle. He delivered his message and fell dead.

The first marathon race of modern times was held in the 1896 Olympic games at Athens, Greece. The most famous marathon race in America is the annual Boston Marathon.

The Steeplechase

The word *steeplechase* was first used to describe a horse race over obstacles in open country. The steeplechase foot race started by accident. In 1850, students from Exeter College, Oxford, England, were watching horses jumping over hedges, water pools, and stone walls in a steeplechase. When the race was over, one rider said, "Next time I would rather go over the obstacle course on human foot." A challenge was taken, and this is how the first modern steeplechase foot race started.

Steeplechase foot racing was first introduced in the United States in 1889.

Today the distance for a steeplechase race is anywhere between one and two miles. The event in the Olympic games is 3,000 meters or about 3,280 yards. The event is run on a track, and the obstacles are man-made fences, walls, hedges, and water holes that each racer must hurdle to successfully complete the course.

Pentathlon

The word *pentathlon* was first introduced by the Greeks in 708 B.C. and became a regular Olympic event. The pentathlon event consists of a contest where one man competes in five different sports. The events for the pentathlon in the early Greek Olympic games were comprised of a run, long jump, discus, javelin, and wrestling. The pentathlon was made a part of the modern Olympic games in 1906, but the five events were changed to include the 200-meter run, 1,500-meter run, discus throw, javelin throw, and the broad jump. The pentathlon was dropped after the 1924 Olympic games, but the Modern Pentathlon was reinstated for men in 1952 (won by Lars Hall of Sweden) and for women in 1964 (won by Irina Press of the U.S.S.R.).

Sports-loving people the world over want to see performances by an all-round athlete. That is what the *decathlon* tries to prove. The word was first used by the ancient Greeks. In the Greek language *deka* means *ten,* and *athos* means struggle or *contest.* Hence the word decathlon means a struggle or competition in ten events to determine the all-round champion athlete of the world.

The decathlon events today are the 100, 400, and 1,500-meter runs; the 110-meter high hurdles; the broad jump and high jump; discus throw and javelin throw; pole vault; and shot-put.

Did you know that the athlete must compete in five events each day during the two days of the decathlon? It is the most grueling and exciting event and usually comes as the climax of the Olympic games.

The decathlon was popular in Ireland in the middle of the nineteenth century. The idea spread to America in 1884, and it is a regular feature of the Amateur Athletic Union (AAU) Championships. It became a permanent part of the Olympic games in 1912. The famous and legendary American Indian, Jim Thorpe, won the first decathlon championship and was honored by King Gustave of Sweden as "the greatest athlete in the world." Unfortunately, he had to surrender the awards because he had played semi-professional baseball.

Cross-country Race

This is a popular race that is usually sponsored in the fall months of the year. It is called *cross-country* because the runners must run a course laid out "across the countryside." Parks and golf courses with some hills are popular cross-country running courses. These races were first popular in England and the Scandinavian countries. The AAU in America sponsored the first cross-country championships in 1890 over a 10,000-meter course (about six miles). The National Collegiate Athletic Association (NCAA) started a cross-country event in 1938. Today many high schools have this event in their yearly track programs. The length of the course is usually about two miles. College cross-country courses vary from three to six miles.

Your Endurance Test

Here is your test to see whether you have good heart and breathing endurance, as well as strength and endurance in your legs. It is one more part of the total Youth Physical Fitness Test prepared by the President's Council on Physical Fitness and Sports.

Take this test on an open field, running track, playground, baseball field, football field, or soccer field.

You do not have to run on a straight course. You can run around the bases of a baseball diamond, around a football or soccer field. Mark a starting line and a finish line 600 yards apart. A partner stands at the finish line with a timing watch.

(a) Take a runner's position behind the starting line.

(b) On the signal, "Ready—go," take off and run!

You can walk part of the way, but the idea is to cover the 600 yards as fast as you can.

600-YARD RUN-WALK (BOYS)

Rating Age—	10	11	12	13	14	15	16	17
			Time in Minutes and Seconds					
Excellent	1:58	1:59	1:52	1:46	1:37	1:34	1:32	1:31
Presidential								
Award	2:12	2:8	2:2	1:53	1:46	1:40	1:37	1:36
Good	2:15	2:11	2:5	1:55	1:48	1:42	1:39	1:38
Satisfactory	2:26	2:21	2:15	2:5	1:57	1:49	1:47	1:45
Poor	2:40	2:33	2:26	2:15	2:5	1:58	1:56	1:54

Key: The 600-yard run-walk is measured in minutes and seconds. The number at the left of the column shows the minutes. The number on the right shows the seconds.

Example: If you are eleven years old and finished this test in 1:59, it means that you covered the distance in one minute and fifty-nine seconds. If you are twelve years old and scored 1:52, you covered the distance in one minute and fifty-two seconds.

If you are under ten years old, use the test as an exercise only and *do not try* to see if you can keep up with the older boys and girls.

600-YARD RUN-WALK (GIRLS)

Rating Age—	10	11	12	13	14	15	16	17
			Time in Minutes and Seconds					
Excellent	2:5	2:13	2:14	2:12	2:9	2:9	2:10	2:11
Presidential Award	2:20	2:24	2:24	2:25	2:22	2:23	2:23	2:27
Good	2:26	2:28	2:27	2:29	2:25	2:26	2:26	2:31
Satisfactory	2:41	2:43	2:42	2:44	2:41	2:40	2:42	2:46
Poor	2:55	2:59	2:58	3:0	2:55	2:52	2:56	3:0

Shoes for Endurance Running

In championship track meets, runners use specially designed shoes for certain races. The short middle-distance runners will use shoes similar to those worn by sprinters. Runners entered in the longer-distance races will use wider spikes on their shoes. Cross-country and marathon runners wear shoes with more padding on the heel. This is done to protect their feet because often they do not run on a smooth, level track.

The starting positions for the shorter middle-distance races are similar to those used for sprints. Some runners even like to use the sprinter's start or half-crouch start for the longer middle-distance races.

For the longer-distance, cross-country and marathon races runners use the *standing start*.

The standing-start position does not require starting blocks or holes on the track. On the standing start you must:

1. "Take your mark" by placing one foot just behind the starting line.

2. Place your other foot in back. Now you are in a comfortable standing stride position.

3. If your right leg is forward, the left arm is bent forward just as in a running position. The hand of your bent right arm is resting slightly at the right hip.

4. On "get set" you get down into a slightly crouched position and bend your knees a little. Hold this body position completely still for two seconds.

STANDING START—FIRST STEP

Middle Distance   Longer Distance

5. On command "go," you take a quick step with the front foot. Follow up fast by driving your arms forward and back along with speedy leg work. After you get into running position on the track, continue into the endurance-running stride.

Endurance-running Stride

Your strides for the shorter middle-distance runs are similar to those for the full-speed sprints. The difference is that your steps are a little slower than those you use for the sprints. In the longer middle distance, your strides are a little slower and shorter, and the body is slightly more erect, while you land on the ball or front part of your feet.

The strides for the longer-distance races require that you drop down slightly on your heels, then rock forward and push off your toes. Your body is more erect than in the middle distance. Take slower and shorter strides, pump your arms forward and back in short relaxed movements to conserve energy. Cross-country runners must use a variety of strides. They are forced to run on a flat surface, then uphill or downhill during the balance of the course. This calls for many quick changes in the runner's stride and body form. When running uphill, you must shorten your strides and lean forward, driving your arms in short, powerful bursts. For downhill running, you simply ease off by lengthening your stride as you coast downhill, with your arms pumping slightly lower and forward. This action helps to conserve energy.

Setting the Right Pace

Did you know that some runners with more ability than others often lose a race because of poor pacing? This means that some runners know how to *distribute their energy* throughout the race by practicing *pace running*.

For example, let's imagine three runners are entered to run the mile event.

1. *Number One Runner,* Eddie, sets a *fast pace* for three-fourths of the race and takes a big lead.

2. *Number Two Runner,* Joey, sets a *slow pace* for three-fourths of the race and is running last, quite a distance back.

3. *Number Three Runner,* Terry, sets an *even pace* at the three-quarter distance and is running between the other runners.

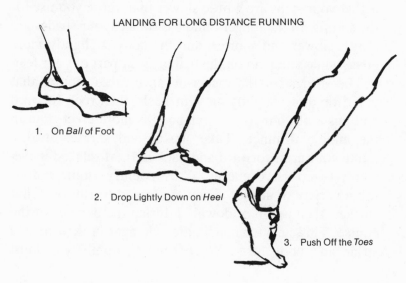

LANDING FOR LONG DISTANCE RUNNING

1. On *Ball* of Foot

2. Drop Lightly Down on *Heel*

3. Push Off the *Toes*

STRIDE AND BODY POSITION IN DISTANCE RUNNING

Body Erect

Ready for Landing

Short Stride

Land on Ball of Foot

High Back Kick

Short Arm Motion

Push-off

Body Leaning More

Shorter, More Vigorous Arm Action

Shorten Stride

Body More Erect

Arms Lower

Lengthen Stride

CROSS-COUNTRY RUNNING *UPHILL*

CROSS-COUNTRY RUNNING *DOWNHILL*

45

Now, all three runners are on the last quarter-mile lap, getting ready for the stretch run to the finish tape.

Eddie is beginning to tire. He has very little energy left, and is barely able to finish with any speed. Joey is beginning to use some of his stored-up energy, and is running with speed, but he is too late to catch up to Terry. Terry ran a smart race. He didn't run too slow or too fast. He saved his energy by pace running, and when he was challenged by Joey, he called on his reserve speed and sprinted away from Joey to win the race easily.

This is one example of what championship runners call pace running. Through training and coaching, each runner will discover how and when he should set a pace for a race.

Later, in another chapter about jogging, you will learn more about energy pacing and coasting for endurance running.

Hints

1. Never take part in endurance races without first having a doctor's examination.

2. If you scored poorly on the 600-yard run-walk test, start right away on a regular daily period of workouts.

3. Even if you made a mark of "excellent" on the test, continue to practice.

4. Breathe freely from both nose and mouth during endurance races.

5. When passing a runner, try to overtake him on the straightaway, just before reaching a curve.

Drills to Improve Your Staying Power

Try these drills with speed and force, depending on your body condition. Start the drills slowly, and as your body "warms up," put more force in your movements. The drills will improve your heart and breathing endurance and give strength and endurance to your legs.

1. Run in place for ten to fifteen seconds. Use low and high knee action and pump your arms vigorously. Rest for ten seconds. Repeat five times.

2. Jump (skip) rope for one minute without stopping. Keep going if you miss a skip. Rest for ten seconds. Do five one-minute jumps with a ten-second rest period between each jump workout.

3. Run at full speed for fifty yards. Walk swiftly for fifteen yards. Repeat this walk-and-run exercise three times without stopping; five times if you have lots of energy left.

4. Walk uphill for five minutes, if a sidewalk or an open field on a hill is available. Rest thirty seconds. Repeat this exercise three times.

5. Walk downhill for five minutes, if a sidewalk or an open field on a hill is available. Rest fifteen seconds. Repeat this exercise three times.

6. Try running up these same hills for one minute. Rest thirty seconds. Repeat five times. Run downhill for two minutes. Rest fifteen seconds. Repeat five times.

7. Jog at an even, slow pace for 200 yards. If you feel good, increase the distance to 300 or 400 yards.

8. Jog at an even, good pace for 100 yards. Walk swiftly for twenty-five yards. Repeat this exercise five times without stopping.

If these exercises are difficult to do, try them at a slower pace and shorten the distances. But get outdoors and get on your feet more often. Do more hiking in the park and in open fields. Use your bicycle often. Take part in more roller- and ice-skating games, and sports in general.

5

Relay Racing
—Teamwork Running

Did you know that relay races are the only real "team" events offered in a Track and Field Championship Meet? This is because all *relay races require two or more runners (teammates) to make up a team to compete in one relay* event against another relay team.

Relay races are thrilling and popular for competitors and fans alike. Usually they are scheduled as a climax, at the end of a track and field meet. They demonstrate a truly teamwork effort in track and field competition.

Relay races offer many boys and girls a chance to compete. *They can be members* of a championship relay team, even when they can't qualify to run in the sprints, distance races, or any of the field events.

History of Relay Racing

Some historians believe that relay races had their beginning when the ancient Greeks held "torch races" during their religious rites. The torch was handed over from one runner to another; each runner had to be careful not to drop it while trying to outrun the rival team.

Other historians believe that relay racing is a modern creation. In fact, the earliest experiments in running with a baton were performed in 1893 by two Americans, J. B.

Ellis and H. L. Gayelin, from the University of Pennsylvania in Philadelphia. Two years later the world-popular mass festival, known as the Penn Relays, was started. The sponsors of this relay hold track and field events for youngsters of school age and performers from all over the world. Another popular festival, called the Drake Relays, was founded by Major John L. Griffith in 1910. In 1908, the relay races were introduced as a regular part of the Olympic games. Today relay-racing meets are sponsored by playgrounds, parks, schools, colleges, and athletic clubs throughout America.

The Different Relay Races

There are many kinds of relay races run at many different distances. Most races are run with four runners on a team, but if the two teams agree, they may run anywhere from two to as many as ten on a relay team. The length of a relay for young people may start as low as twenty-five yards, while the distance for championship meets may go up to a four-mile relay race. Here are some examples:

SPRINT RELAYS. These are the shorter-distance runs for each four members of a relay team. A 440-yard sprint relay race requires that each of the four members shall run 110 yards. ($4 \times 110 = 440$ yards)

MIDDLE-DISTANCE RELAYS. Races of distances beyond the sprint distances and shorter than the longer distances. A two-mile middle-distance relay race requires each of the four members to run 880 yards (one-half mile). (4×880 yards $= 2$ miles)

DISTANCE RELAYS. Often called *long-distance relays*. A four-mile distance relay race requires each of the four members to run one mile. (4×1 mile $= 4$ miles)

SPRINT MEDLEY RELAYS. Got the name *medley* because team members run different distances to complete one race. A 660-yard medley relay race requires the first runner to run 220 yards; the second runner 110 yards; the third runner 110 yards; and the fourth runner 220 yards. (220+110+110+220 = 660 yards)

SHUTTLE HURDLE RELAYS. These are named *shuttle* because the runners race in a "back-and-forth" direction on the track. One-half of the relay team, two members, are lined up on one end of the track facing the other one-half of the team members (two) at the opposite end. One starting runner from each team runs at a time. No other runner leaves his position until he is touched on the shoulder by his teammate. They keep running and jumping over hurdles "back and forth" until all four team members run the required distance. A 480-yard shuttle, low-hurdles relay race requires each four members to run 120 yards. (4 × 120 yards = 480 yards)

SHUTTLE "FLAT" RELAYS. Races that are run without hurdles. They are run either on the "flat" track or grass portion of the field. A 220-yard shuttle flat relay race requires that each of the four members run fifty-five yards. (4 × 55 yards = 220 yards)

MAKE-UP RELAYS. These are races sponsored by different groups interested in foot racing. The relay races might cover distances from one city or town to another. Sometimes they are run from one park or school to the center of town, or from one neighborhood to another.

The Baton

Before the baton was invented, members of a relay team running in the same direction would tag the next runner on the hand to signal the start of his portion of the race. This caused a good deal of argument about

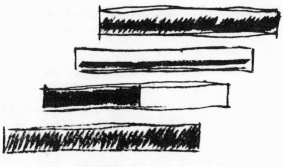

BATONS

whether or not the runner was actually tagged. Today the rules state that a baton must be used for certain relay races.

An official baton is shaped like a piece of tubing or a broom handle. It must not be more than one foot long, not weigh less than one and three-fourths ounces, and must be four and three-fourths inches in circumference (round).

The batons are made of many different kinds of material, such as plastic, aluminum, wood, hard cardboard; they are often painted in school or college colors.

Many races may be won by skillful baton handling, so let's learn about the rules and methods of passing the baton.

Rule for Passing Baton

Did you know that in relay races where a baton is used, the baton must be given to the next runner within a specific area marked in each lane on the track? The first runner in the race starts with the baton. He must then run a specific distance and give it to the next member of his relay team. The runners continue to run a certain distance and to pass the baton to a waiting teammate. This goes on until the last runner carries the baton across the finish line of the race.

RELAY PASSING OR EXCHANGE ZONE. The area marked on the track where each runner gives the baton to the next runner is known as the *relay passing* or *exchange zone*. This zone is twenty-two yards long. There are finish lines in each lane to signal the runners that they have completed their portion of the race. This same line is the starting line for the waiting member of the team to receive the baton. Lines are drawn eleven yards before and eleven yards beyond the finish and starting lines. The passing or handling of the baton to the next runner *must be made within any portion of this twenty-two-yard area.*

In the shorter-distance relay races, runners waiting to receive the baton may take a position eleven yards in front of the first line of the exchange zone. This gives each runner a chance to get a good running start before taking the baton from his teammate. The baton *must* be passed to the receiving runner before he leaves the end of the exchange zone.

For longer-distance relay races, the runners waiting to receive the baton must always start their position in the exchange zone, and complete the baton passing within this zone.

The baton must *be passed* or *handed* and *not thrown* to the next runner. Runners are disqualified if the baton is

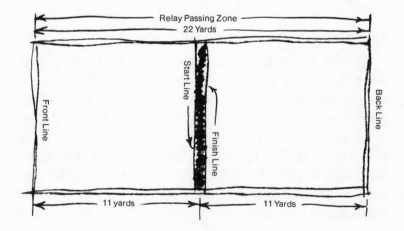

passed outside (before or after) the twenty-two-yard passing zone.

If the baton is dropped in the exchange zone, either of the two runners may pick it up and continue the race as planned. If the baton is dropped outside the passing zone, the runner dropping the baton must pick it up and continue to run.

After passing the baton to his partner, the runner should stand still or jog straight ahead in his own lane to avoid bothering runners from the other team. If the baton passers are on the inside or outside lanes, they should step off the track immediately after completing the baton pass.

Know these rules. They will all help you and your relay-team members with races.

Now let's find out how you can learn to make the different relay passes just like the champions do.

Passing the Baton

Split-second timing—this is what you see when a runner is passing the baton to a teammate running in the same direction. Baton passing is where teamwork and practice help win relay races.

On your relay team there will be three baton passes made in a race. The first runner passes to number two runner; number two runner to number three; and number three runner to number four, who crosses the final finish line. This is like a passing and receiving game throughout the race.

How does the first runner on the starting line hold the baton? What starting position does he take? How do the other runners line up on the track? These are some of the skills that must be learned in a baton-passing relay race.

First Runner in Starting Position

The first runner of the relay team has an additional responsibility that other runners do not have. He must know how to hold the baton from a regular crouch or sprinter's-start position. There is a rule for the first runner to start with a baton in his hand: *The baton must not touch the ground on or past the starting line.*

Each runner must be sure that he holds the baton in a way that is safe and comfortable for him. At the start of a relay, make certain that you are holding the baton securely. If you drop the baton at the starting signal, it can lose the race for your team.

Here are the most popular methods the first runners use to hold the baton on the starting line:

1. Grasp the baton with the third finger only. The thumb, second, fourth, and fifth fingers are stretched out touching the ground behind the starting line.

2. Another method is to grasp the baton with the third and fourth fingers only. The thumb, second, and fifth fingers are stretched out touching the ground behind the starting line.

3. Still another style is to grasp the baton with the second or index finger only, with the thumb, third, fourth, and fifth fingers stretched out.

4. Some young beginners wish to grip the baton with all four fingers because they feel safer. This means that only your thumb and knuckles touch the ground behind the starting line.

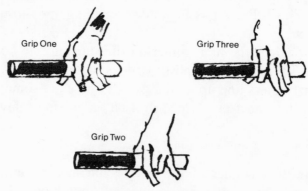

Grip One

Grip Three

Grip Two

FIRST RUNNER GRIPS HOLDING BATON

Now let's get ready and try still another grip—one that is most popular with young champions. Use one of the others only if you believe it is best for you.

YOUR FAVORITE BATON GRIP AT START OF RACE. Take your regular starting position. Hold the baton in the hand you will use to pass to the next runner. Grip it at one end so at least one-half is free for the next runner to receive it. Keep the third, fourth, and fifth fingers wrapped around the baton. The thumb and index or second finger are stretched apart touching directly behind the starting line forming a *V*. Your other hand is in a regular sprint starting position.

When you are in a "get set" position, the front (free) portion of the baton will be past the starting line, but *not touching the ground*. This is prevented because your baton hand is resting on your thumb and second finger and, also, slightly on the knuckles of the fingers wrapped around the baton.

On the "go" signal, take off and drive forward toward the second runner, ready to make a smooth baton pass.

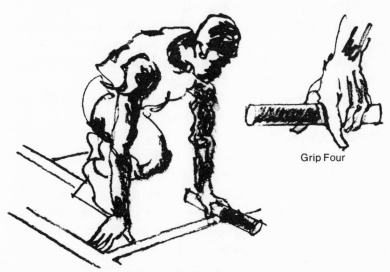

Grip Four

FIRST RUNNER USING GRIP FOUR

There are many ways for relay runners to pass or receive the baton. All techniques of passing and receiving the baton fall into two groups—*visual passes* and *blind passes*.

BLIND PASSES. Used in short or sprint relay distances. The *visual passes* are mostly used in the longer-distance relays. Blind passes are also called *non-visual passes*. They are given this name because the runners receiving the baton are not watching the baton when it is passed to them.

VISUAL PASSES. Those passes used when the runners receiving the baton are watching it being passed to them.

Before making a baton pass you must know what position the runners of the relay team will take on the track.

Position of Runners on Track

There are several ways the runners of a relay team take their positions on the track. Here is one of the most popular ways the four members of your relay team will line up on the first or inside lane of the track.

Each runner will sprint fifty yards to make up the total distance of a 200-yard relay race.

The *first runner* takes his starting position with the baton in his right hand, as close as possible to the left side of the lane.

The *second runner* takes a position fifty yards down the track, as close as possible to the right side of the same lane. He is ready to receive the baton in his left hand.

The *third runner,* fifty yards more down on the track, takes a position as close as possible to the left side of the lane. He is ready to receive the baton with his right hand.

The *fourth runner* takes a position close to the right side of the lane. He is ready to receive the baton with his

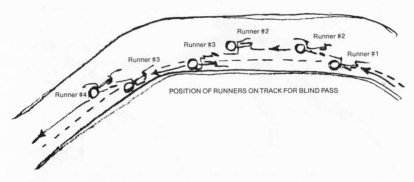

Runner #2

Runner #3

Runner #2

Runner #3

Runner #1

Runner #4

POSITION OF RUNNERS ON TRACK FOR BLIND PASS

left hand while sprinting the remaining fifty yards across the finish line. Remember that all four runners stay in their own lane during the race.

By taking these positions for this kind of sprint relay race, each runner will find that he *passes the baton with the same hand he received it in from the runner before him.*

In other words, the number one and three runners, located at the left side of the lane, carry the baton with the right hand. The number two and four runners, at the right side of the lane, carry the baton with the left hand.

Now let's get ready to make an actual blind pass for a sprint relay!

Making the Blind Pass

This kind of pass calls for real teamwork and practice if it is going to work smoothly. By not looking back, the sprinters receiving the baton are able to keep up their rapid and smooth sprint-running form.

The *starting runner* is off! Holding the baton in his right hand, he sprints full speed as close along the left-lane line as possible, but does not step on the line.

The *second runner* is waiting close to the right side of the lane, eleven yards before the front line of the passing zone. He stands with his body leaning forward and feet and knees pointing straight ahead. He keeps his head slightly turned to the left and watches the runner getting

SECOND RUNNER MAKING LEFT-HAND BLIND PASS

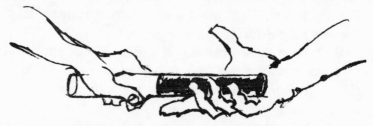

CLOSE-UP OF HAND POSITION (BLIND PASS)

closer. When the runner advances to within twenty feet of him, he begins to sprint straight ahead, without looking back.

The runner with the baton has now reached the passing-zone area. He is catching up to the second runner. The second runner is sprinting, with his body leaning low and forward. Both sprinters are now in position and ready to make the pass.

Here is what happens. The second runner on the forward pumping motion of his left arm begins to get his left fingers together, with the thumb stretched out (away from fingers). On the back pumping motion he "whips" his left arm back along the side of his hip and parallel or even to the ground. The elbow and palm of the hand are facing up, thumb pointing inward, and fingers pointing back. The receiving runner is ready with a steady hand and makes a "target" for the baton passer. *The baton passer is responsible for placing the baton in the hand of the receiver.*

With perfect timing the first runner stretches or pushes his right arm slightly above the height of the receiver's left hand. With a quick downward wrist motion, he places the baton in the open left hand of the receiver.

This action takes place within the passing zone, with both runners sprinting ahead with their bodies leaning forward.

The remaining runners in this type of relay race use the same skills for passing and receiving the baton. This is like a game of *sprint-pass-receive, sprint-pass-receive* with no slow-up action at all.

Making the Visual Pass

This is the baton pass that you use when the passer runs a longer distance than in the sprint relays.

The runner making the pass is tired when he reaches the next runner who is to receive the baton. This is why the receiver keeps his eyes on the baton until he has it in his hand.

In these relays it is the *responsibility of the receiver to see that a good baton pass is made.*

Even though the visual pass is a little slower than the blind pass, it is *safer.*

Most first runners on a distance relay team will take a standing-start position instead of the sprinter's-start position.

Let's begin by having the first runner in a standing-start position behind the starting line. He holds an end portion of the baton in his left hand. It is a mile distance relay. Each runner must cover 440 yards.

The *first runner* is off! He runs as fast as he can while pacing himself—thus he is not tired before reaching the passing zone.

The *second runner* is standing just inside the front line of the passing zone. He turns his head, looking over his

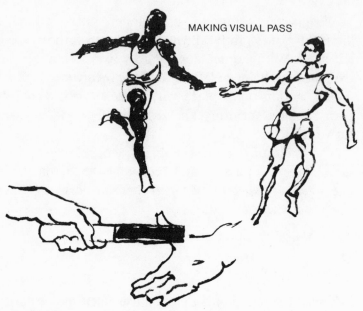

MAKING VISUAL PASS

CLOSE-UP OF HAND POSITION (VISUAL PASS)

right shoulder. The left (front) foot is pointed straight ahead. The right (back) foot is slightly turned to the right.

When the baton passer reaches a marked spot about fifteen feet before the passing zone, the baton receiver begins to move. He straightens his body and turns his right arm back slightly to the right at a height of about four to six inches above the hips. The elbow faces downward. The palm of his hand is facing upward, fingers together with the thumb pointed toward the rear. Driving off with the right foot, he takes his first step forward with the left foot.

The first runner reaches the front line of the passing zone. He uses just about the same baton-passing technique as for the sprint relay. He stretches his left arm forward with the baton in hand.

The two runners have planned to time the pass so it will take place just before the center line of the passing zone.

60

POSITION OF RUNNERS FOR VISUAL PASS

As they meet, the pass receiver keeps his eyes on the baton while he is on the move. He *grabs* the baton with a firm right-hand grip from the passer's hand as it moves downward, and then starts his pace running toward the next pass receiver. The remaining runners perform the same pass-receiving action.

For this kind of baton-passing, the receivers must learn to shift the baton from the right hand to the left hand to be ready for the next pass. In other words, *all runners will pass with the left hand and receive with the right hand.* Some coaches prefer to have the first runner start with the baton in his right hand. In this case, the second, third, and fourth runners will turn their heads, looking over the left shoulder, and receive the baton with the left hand.

Shifting Baton from Right to Left Hand on the Run

It is important to change the baton from your right to left hand without slowing up your running stride or dropping the baton.

After receiving one end of the baton with your right hand, quickly bring both hands directly in front of you, slightly above your hips. Grasp the baton firmly with the left hand and speed into your regular running stride. If the baton is received with the left hand, you will shift it from the left to right hand while on the run.

61

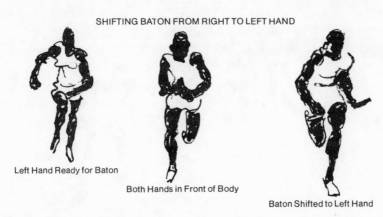

Left Hand Ready for Baton

Both Hands in Front of Body

Baton Shifted to Left Hand

All this action takes place anywhere during the first five strides after receiving the baton.

Other Baton Passes

Here are other kinds of baton passes that some relay teams like to use. They may be done as blind passes or visual passes. Be careful! Practice and use only the ones that are safest for you. Later, when you grow older and practice with a regular relay team, you will find that a certain kind of pass may be more successful for your team.

1. The receiver rests the finger tips of his right hand on his hip, with the thumb pointed forward and his elbow out. The hand is now in a cupped position. The passer stretches his left arm forward and places the baton downward into the receiver's cupped hand.

2. The receiver rests the thumb of his right hand on his hip, with fingers pointed downward and elbow facing slightly to the rear. The passer stretches his left arm forward with an upward motion and places the baton in the receiver's right hand.

3. The receiver stretches his right arm back, with palm facing out and thumb slightly upward. The elbow is facing toward the body. The passer stretches his left arm

forward, holding the baton in an upright position instead of forward. The receiver grasps the top portion of the baton.

4. The receiver stretches his right arm back and slightly downward to hip level. The thumb and fingers are pointing down, with the palm facing the rear. The passer stretches his left arm forward with an upward motion and places the baton in the receiver's right hand.

Medley Relay Baton Passing

Did you know that members of a medley relay team may use both the visual and blind passing during one race? This is done because certain members of a medley relay team are required to run only a short distance to make the baton pass. This runner is fresh, so the receiver will be ready for a blind pass—just as in the sprint relay race.

Other members of the medley relay team must run a longer distance to make a baton pass. These runners are tired, so the receivers will be ready for visual passes—just as in the distance relay race.

Shuttle Relay Races

Shuttle relay races are often the most popular events of many sponsored track and field programs in the country. There are special shuttle relays for youngsters, for players on a football team, and for the regulation shuttle relay championship meets.

Most shuttle relay races for young boys and girls are known as the *shuttle "flat" relay races*. The *shuttle hurdle relay races* are also sponsored for older boys and girls. You will learn all about the hurdling skills later in this book. Otherwise, the running skills are the same for the shuttle hurdle and flat relay races.

Rules for Shuttle "Flat" Relay Running. Shuttle "flat" relay races are run on either the flat track or grass portion of the field.

There are four members on a regulation shuttle relay team. The team is divided into two pairs, and each pair (2 runners) faces the other. You may have more runners on a team if agreed upon by the other team. If you have ten on a team, you will have five in each group facing the other.

It is a good idea to line up by having the odd numbers in one group and the even numbers in the other. Numbers one and three on one side of the starting line face numbers two and four behind the other starting line. If each runner must sprint twenty-five yards, there will be two starting-finishing lines twenty-five yards apart.

The teams must decide what method they will use to signal when each runner must begin to run his portion of the race. Here are the different methods the teams may agree upon:

1. The number-one runner on each team starts the race with a baton in his hand. He runs and passes it to number-two runner, who then will pass it to number three. Number three passes it to number four, who crosses the final finish line. *Many coaches do not recommend the use of the baton-shuttle relay pass,* for many runners find it difficult to receive the baton from the passer who is racing toward him at full speed.

2. The *tag-shuttle relay method of signaling the runner to begin his portion of the race is the most popular for young people.* This is done with each runner taking the sprinter's position on the starting blocks. The first runner sprints toward the second runner, who is in a "get set" position. Upon being tagged on the right shoulder by the first runner, he dashes toward runner number three, who is waiting in a "get set" position. This continues until the last member of the shuttle relay team is tagged and crosses

the finish line. In championship meets, an inspector stands at each starting line to act as a judge. This inspector sees that the runner does not leave the starting line before he is tagged.

3. If the shuttle relay teams use a standing-start position, each runner must tag the next runner's right hand before he begins to run. In some championship meets, the runners in a standing-start position hook one arm around a portable post. When it is touched or tagged by the previous runner, he takes off to touch the next runner's arm around the post. This helps to prevent a runner from leaving the starting line ahead of time.

Relay-racing Strategy

Which of the four members of a relay team should run first, second, third, or fourth? Who should run the sprints in a medley relay race? What runners should use the blind pass?

These are only a few of the questions for which a coach or team captain will need the answers. The more information that is known about each runner, the wiser the race will be run. This is known as good strategy. Here are some questions whose answers you should know for the practice or use of good relay-racing strategy:

1. Which member runs best when behind? (Some become discouraged and do not run as well, while others take the challenge to catch or pass the leading runner.)

2. Which member runs best when in front?

3. Who is the fastest starter?

4. Which two runners make a speedy and smooth baton pass?

5. Are some runners best when assigned to run in certain lanes?

6. Who are the longer-distance and good pace runners?

7. Who runs the track curve best?

8. Who is the strongest finisher?

Once this information is known about the runners, each coach or captain must decide in which order they will run.

ORDER OF RUNNERS FOR SPRINT RELAY. One of the most popular strategies used for the sprint relay is to have the *strongest* finisher *run last* (number four). He must have the ability to hold a lead, or to catch up and pass his opponents.

The best starter and second-fastest runner usually "leads off" the race by running *first*.

The slowest sprinter on the team runs *second*. If he loses ground to his opponent, the next two runners have a chance to catch up.

The *third* runner is known as a strong runner, not necessarily the fastest.

ORDER OF RUNNERS FOR MEDLEY RELAY. A similar strategy of deciding who will run first, second, third, and fourth is used for the medley relay race. The important differences are to assign the short-distance portions of the race to the best sprinters, and the longer distances to runners with stamina.

ORDER OF RUNNERS FOR DISTANCE RELAYS. For the longer-distance relays, the fastest man is usually assigned to run last. He is also known as the "anchor man." The second fastest man is assigned to run in the third spot. The slowest runners are assigned the number one and two positions. Some coaches feel that this strategy allows the last two runners to make up for any ground lost by the first two runners.

Regardless of the system used to assign runners their positions, it is best that different combinations be tried. Runners and coaches must, also, consider the weather, the line-up of the opposing team, and the type of track used.

Drills

BATON-PASSING DRILLS. Make a baton from a piece of broomstick, tree branch, or cardboard roll.

1. Stand in front of a mirror. From a stationary position, go through the actual motions of a sprint passer and receiver. Now try the movements of the distant (visual) baton passer and receiver. Try it with a teammate.

2. In front of a mirror, practice shifting the baton from one hand to the other hand, ready to make the pass. Practice this drill while walking. Then practice while jogging and running.

3. Practice the actual motions of the different kinds of baton-receiving skills with a teammate in the gymnasium or open field; then practice with four members of your relay team.

4. Walk through this same drill with each runner about six feet apart. Check on the signals when each runner moves forward for the blind pass; also for the visual pass.

5. Mark off the twenty-two feet baton-passing-zone area. You will need three of these zones if you practice with four runners. Now, jog through the same drill as in number four above. Start putting some speed in your baton-passing and baton-receiving routines.

6. *Run* through the same drill as in number five. Work for smooth passing and receiving. Check to see that all four runners are working as a team.

7. Make up your own relay races. Start with each member of the team running twenty-five yards. Increase the distance only when the runners are in good condition. Use a watch with a second hand to see how you improve.

SHUTTLE RUN TEST. This is another test sponsored by the President's Council on Physical Fitness and Sports. It can be used as a drill. This test will measure your speed, body agility, and flexibility of the hip joints.

Mark two parallel lines thirty feet apart. Place two wooden blocks (about the size of blackboard erasers) just behind the far line. Have a partner check your running time with a stopwatch or any watch that can mark the seconds and tenths of seconds.

(a) Take a running stance behind the starting line.

(b) On the signal, "go," run swiftly toward the blocks. Pick one up, race back, and set the block behind the starting line.

(c) Without stopping, run for the other block, pick it up, and speed back across the starting line without stopping to put this second block down.

Take two trials in this test. Mark down the time for your fastest run as your score.

SHUTTLE RUN (BOYS)

Rating	Age—	10	11	12	13	14	15	16	17
		Time in seconds and tenths of a second							
Excellent		10.0	10.0	9.8	9.5	9.3	9.1	9.0	8.9
Presidential Award		10.4	10.3	10.0	9.9	9.6	9.4	9.2	9.1
Good		10.5	10.4	10.2	10.0	9.8	9.5	9.3	9.2
Satisfactory		11.0	10.9	10.7	10.4	10.0	9.8	9.7	9.6
Poor		11.5	11.3	11.1	10.9	10.5	10.1	10.0	10.0

Key to measure running time: The number to the left of the decimal point is seconds. The number to the right of the decimal point is tenths of a second.

Example: If you are eleven years old and ran the race for a score of excellent, your time was ten seconds. If you are under ten years old, practice this drill to improve your skills, but do *not* worry about the time.

SHUTTLE RUN (GIRLS)

Rating	Age—	10	11	12	13	14	15	16	17
		Time in seconds and tenths of a second							
Excellent		10.0	10.0	10.0	10.0	10.0	10.0	10.0	10.0
Presidential Award		10.8	10.6	10.5	10.5	10.4	10.5	10.4	10.4
Good		11.0	10.9	10.8	10.6	10.5	10.7	10.6	10.5
Satisfactory		11.5	11.4	11.3	11.1	11.0	11.1	11.0	11.0
Poor		12.0	12.0	11.9	11.8	11.5	11.6	11.5	11.5

Try this shuttle-run distance with a regular four-member shuttle relay team without the blocks. Have two runners of each team behind the thirty feet starting lines. Have a starter give the "go" signal for the first runner to run swiftly toward the second team man. Complete the race with number-four runner crossing the finish line. Check the watch to see how fast your team ran.

Shuttle relay drills are fun and healthy for any age level. If your team is in good condition, increase the distance of the race. Practice on the smooth "tagging" of the shoulder, hand, or post. See that the runner does not take off before the tag.

6

Hurdle Racing

Today the hurdle event is popular for spectators and competitors alike. This is because everyone enjoys the sight of an athlete running with speed and also "hurdling" over barriers to win a race. Young athletes run the hurdles in meets sponsored by schools, parks, and sports clubs.

Hurdling is a track event. Speed runners usually enter in a track and field competition in both sprints and hurdles events. Younger boys and girls should get an early start to learn the skills of hurdling.

Construction and Height of Hurdles

The hurdles are also known as *barriers* or *obstacles*. They are put in the way of the runner and he must clear them by "hurdling" in order to reach the finish line. Each hurdle is placed carefully on the ground so that the base and bar on which it stands face the runner.

The hurdles for championship events must be made of metal or wood material. They consist of two vertical uprights. The uprights must be joined together by one or more crossbars to form a rectangular frame. The top crossbar must be of wood two and three-fourths inches wide and a minimum of forty-two inches long.

The surface of the crossbar which faces the starting line (or runners) must be white, with at least two painted black vertical or diagonal stripes. This is necessary so that the athletes can easily see the top crossbar.

Many hurdles are constructed so they can be adjusted to the heights needed for the different hurdle races.

The *low hurdles* for high schools and colleges are thirty inches high. The *intermediate hurdles* are thirty-six inches high and are used for the Olympic games, college, and Amateur Athletic Union events. The *high hurdles* for high school are thirty-nine inches in height, and for colleges and international competition are forty-two inches high.

Hurdle heights for young boys and girls range from eighteen to thirty inches.

CHAMPIONSHIP HURDLE

The most common hurdle races for championship meets are the 120-yard high hurdles; 180-yard low hurdles; 220-yard low hurdles; and 440-yard intermediate height hurdles.

Girls' championship events start from fifty yards and go to about 220 yards.

Indoor distances range from fifty to seventy yards, depending on the facilities available.

Distances for young boys and girls may vary from forty to 100 yards.

Number of Hurdles Used in Race

The number of hurdles a runner must clear in a race depends on the distance of the race. There are as many as ten hurdles in the longer championship hurdle distance races.

The number of hurdles used for races among youngsters varies from four to eight, depending on the distance to be run.

Hurdles Chart for Young Athletes

Young boys and girls should study the chart that follows. It gives them the correct height for the hurdles, distance between hurdles, and length of the race for the different age groups.

Rules for Hurdling

1. The runner must go over the hurdle with his entire body and remain in his own lane.

2. The runner cannot go around the hurdle.

3. The runner cannot interfere with a hurdler in another lane.

4. A runner cannot purposely knock down any hurdle in his lane. There is no penalty if one or more hurdles are knocked down by accident.

HURDLES CHART FOR YOUNG ATHLETES

Age Group	Hurdle Height in Inches	Number of Hurdles	Starting Line to 1st Hurdle (Feet & Inches)	Distance Between Hurdles (Feet & Inches)	Last Hurdle to Finish Line (Feet & Inches)	Distance of Race in Yards
11 years and under boys and girls (beginners)	18 or 24	4	22 feet	26 ft. 3 in.	23 ft. 3 in.	50 yds.
11 years and under boys and girls	30	6	33 ft. 4 in.	22 ft. 3 in.	35 ft. 5 in.	60 yds.
13 years and under boys	30	8	39 ft. 4 in.	26 ft. 3 in.	39 ft. 4 in.	87½ yds.
girls	30	6	36 ft. 4 in.	14 ft. 3 in.	22 ft. 5 in.	60 yds.

It is important to know that in hurdling a runner thinks of *running* over the hurdles and not *jumping* over them. This means you must practice good sprinting form while approaching and going over the hurdles.

Youngsters do not compete in the high hurdles until they are older and bigger. The high hurdles will force you to *jump* over the hurdles and cause you to lose hurdling form. The low hurdles will give you a good chance to run the hurdles like a young champion sprinter.

Here are some of the techniques a young hurdler must learn:

1. The position of the feet at the starting blocks.
2. The running form in leaving the starting blocks and just before reaching the first hurdle, and between each hurdle.
3. The number of strides to take before reaching the first hurdle, and between each hurdle.
4. The positions of your arms, legs, and body as you approach and clear the hurdle.

Let's take these points one at a time so you will be better prepared for real hurdle racing.

Hurdler's Starting Position

A *right-footed* hurdler or football kicker should place his left foot on the front starting block. (*Left-footed* hurdler places right foot on front block.) This means that you will make use of your left (strong) foot for driving the right (front) foot over the hurdle with great power.

This also means that the right-footed hurdler must take an *even number of strides (steps)* to get the right foot over the first hurdle. Should a right-footed hurdler reach the first hurdle in an *odd number of strides,* it will be necessary for him to reverse his foot position at the starting block. His right foot, instead of the left, will be on the front starting block.

Try to remember that the "lead leg" in hurdling means the leg that goes over the hurdle first. The other leg is known as the "trailing leg" or "takeoff leg." The "takeoff spot" is a point on the track directly in front of the hurdle. This is the point where your takeoff leg makes the last step to push the lead leg over the hurdle.

Now let's see how you run toward the first hurdle.

Strides to First Hurdle

Your speed, strength, skill, and size will determine how many strides you need to reach the first hurdle.

Once you know the distance between the starting line and the first hurdle, you should practice running the distance without hurdles. Count the number of strides it would take you to cover the distance. Then stick to the number you feel most comfortable taking.

If you are running the fifty-yard hurdle race, as shown on your study chart, the distance from the starting line to the first hurdle is twenty-two feet. Will it take you four, six, or eight (even number) strides to get your right foot

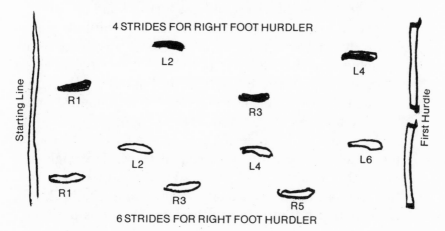

over the first hurdle? If it takes you an even number of strides, you will have started with the left foot at the front starting block. Don't worry about how many strides it takes you to reach the hurdles. The important thing to remember is to run with a sprinter's stride and to take the hurdles with form and timing.

Approaching and Clearing First Hurdle

Let us decide, as you approach the first hurdle, that you are going to make a right-footed clearance of the hurdle. How will you approach the hurdle? How will you clear it? How will you land after clearing the hurdle? As a beginner, you should practice on the eighteen-inch hurdles. Later on, as you develop your form and ability, you can try to use the regulation size—twenty-four-inch—hurdle.

APPROACH. Your eyes are focused on top of the hurdle as you approach it. Concentrate on your sprinting form. You reach the takeoff spot with your left trailing leg about three to five feet in front of the hurdle. Some youngsters can make a good takeoff from six to seven feet in front of the hurdle. Use the distance most comfortable to you.

CLEARING HURDLE. When your left trailing leg reaches the takeoff spot, lift the right knee forward and up just as you would in a regular sprint stride, but a little higher. Push the right foot forward so the leg is forced to straighten out. The toe of the right lead foot points forward and up just before it reaches the hurdle.

The trailing or takeoff foot gives you the upward and forward drive for the body to clear the hurdle.

As soon as the right lead leg clears the hurdle, the trailing or takeoff leg is quickly brought forward. Straighten (extend) the upper thigh outward and bend the knee so that the toes and the knee are pointing out. The back of the trailing-leg foot is facing the rear. Hold this position

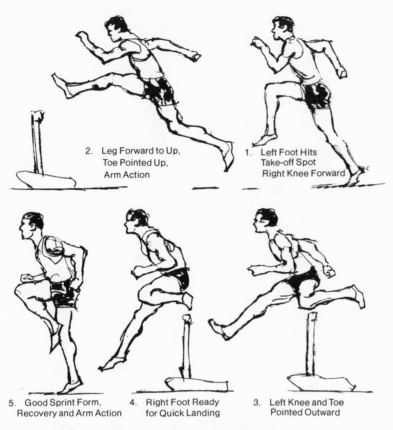

2. Leg Forward to Up,
   Toe Pointed Up,
   Arm Action

1. Left Foot Hits
   Take-off Spot
   Right Knee Forward

5. Good Sprint Form,
   Recovery and Arm Action

4. Right Foot Ready
   for Quick Landing

3. Left Knee and Toe
   Pointed Outward

FORM CLEARING THE LOW HURDLE

momentarily to make certain the trailing-leg knee and foot do not hit the top of the hurdle.

During this action the *arm position* helps to give you good body balance. With a right lead leg, the left arm drives forward from the shoulder just as if you were reaching down toward the foot of the lead leg. The right arm is thrust in a regular sprinter's position close to your right side and slightly back. This action helps to keep you from twisting your body to one side while clearing the hurdle. The idea is to keep your shoulders straight and bend your body slightly forward throughout the hurdling action, so that you can continue on to the next hurdle.

FIRST-STEP LANDING. Your right lead leg should strike the ground as quickly as possible after it clears the hurdle. You do this by a "snapping" action downward on the ball of your lead foot, with toes pointing straight ahead.

The trailing foot is "floating" past the hurdle, to be brought down quickly with a good forward stride in front of the lead foot. Your body is bent slightly forward on the landing and first step. Good recovery with a vigorous sprinter's arm action helps you to pick up your balance and speed for the next hurdle.

Strides between Hurdles

You are now sprinting toward the next hurdle, which is a distance away of twenty-six feet and three inches, according to your fifty-yard hurdles race on the chart. You again plan to use the right leg as the lead leg going over the hurdle. This means you must take an odd number of strides between each hurdle.

Youngsters take from five to seven strides to cover the distance to the next hurdle. After much practice, you will find the number of strides best for you.

Once you have cleared the first hurdle, you must make a fast recovery into a sprinter's action. Now begin to set your eyes on the top crossbar of the next hurdle, and repeat the good form you used in the previous hurdle.

Finish of Race

Once you have cleared the last hurdle, finish the race just as a sprinter would. Turn on all the speed you have and cross the finish line as if you still had about ten more yards to run.

Does this look like a lot of work? A lot of rules to remember? A lot of skills to learn? Hurdling is difficult, but once you develop the proper skills, you will find it a lot of fun. Here are hints you can follow and drills you can actually practice—alone or with friends.

1. Start your first practices on grass surfaces when possible.

2. Stick with low-height hurdles practice.

3. Stop your hurdles practice when you begin to feel tired.

4. Do warm-up and stretching exercises before actual competition in the hurdle events.

5. Get immediate treatment if you are injured.

6. Clearing the low hurdle is not a jump upward. It is more like a regular forward sprint stride, but just a little higher.

Drills and Exercises

Hurdlers specialize in their own kind of exercise and drills. These not only help to improve skill, but put one in better physical condition.

HURDLER'S EXERCISE. Sit on the floor with legs together. Slide the right leg around to the rear, keeping the knee bent, and point the toes outward. While in this position, stretch forward as far as possible and touch your left toe with your right hand. Stretch your left arm toward the rear. You are now in the position of a hurdler. Bend forward a few times toward the front leg and keep that front leg straight.

Try this in the opposite direction, with the left foot forward and right leg toward the rear. You should feel a tremendous stretch in the muscles of the forward leg.

HURDLER'S STRETCHER. Set up a hurdle, crossbar, or box of the same height as the height of your hips. Stand next to it with your right leg and hip touching the hurdle. Grasp the hurdle with the right hand for support. Lift your right leg upward and rest it on the hurdle.

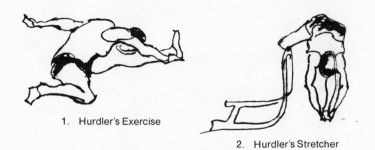

1. Hurdler's Exercise

2. Hurdler's Stretcher

3. Lead Leg Exercise

Now bend to your waist and try touching your left foot with both hands. Make a few short bends up and down. You can actually feel the muscles stretching.

Do the same exercise with the left leg resting on the hurdle.

If you do not have a hurdle or box, use an old chair or sofa, but make sure it is safe and that you have your parents' permission.

LEAD-LEG EXERCISE. This is done the same as the last exercise (hurdler's stretcher), but this time you face the hurdle and rest the ball of the right foot on the hurdle. Lean forward slightly with your left hand stretched toward the toe of the lead foot.

Try the same exercise with the left foot resting on the hurdle.

There are many more exercises. It is always a good idea to do bending and stretching exercises. Toe-touching, knee-raising, running-in-place, and trunk-twisting are very good exercises to help you become a successful hurdler. And you must practice, practice, practice.

To improve your hurdling skills, you should practice the simple drills first, then work up to the advanced drills. Here are some drills you will want to try before you actually attempt running in a real hurdle race.

1. Take a regular sprinter's start and run with speed for ten yards, pretending to keep your eyes on an imaginary hurdle.

2. Draw or place a marker (obstacle) the width of a hurdle crossbar on the ground twenty-two feet from the starting line. This is the distance between the starting line and the first hurdle for the fifty-yard hurdle race. The markers can be made of strips of cardboard, newspapers, tape, or flat sticks. Take your starting position for a right lead foot to hurdle over the obstacle (marker) on the ground. Begin your sprint and check the length and number of strides it took you to go over the first obstacle. How was your form going over the ground marker?

3. Place a second marker on the ground twenty-six feet, three inches past the first marker. This is the distance between the first and second hurdle for the fifty-yard hurdle race. Start your sprint. Clear the first ground marker with the right lead foot. Continue the sprint and check the length and number of strides it took to clear the second marker with a right-foot lead.

4. Look back at the hurdles chart earlier in this chapter. Place markers on the ground for the number of hurdles listed for the race. Then practice correct timing and form until you feel confident you can begin to hurdle over higher obstacles.

5. Place two shoe boxes, small stands, bundles of newspapers and magazines, bricks, or adjustable hurdles on the ground. They should be set the width apart of a regular hurdle crossbar. In place of a hurdle crossbar, use one end of a piece of cloth, paper, gauze, or flat stick on top of each box, or bricks, or whatever you use. A piece of tape will hold the ends in place. Start your prac-

tice by having the height of the artificial crossbar at about twelve inches, then raise the height to eighteen inches. When you feel comfortable, add the number of artificial hurdles you need for a regular race, as listed on the chart. Then gradually raise the height to twenty-four inches and *no higher* than thirty inches.

6. If you have trouble lifting the trailing back leg over the crossbar, here is the drill for you. Place the height of the practice or real hurdle at a height of twenty-four or thirty inches. *Walk* down beside the hurdle. As you are about to reach the hurdle, step in front and slightly to the side of the hurdle with the lead leg. The lead leg does not go over the crossbar. Allow only the trailing leg to clear the hurdle. After this, try *jogging,* and then go over the hurdle the same way. Then sprint and clear the hurdle. Do this several times until you develop your timing and form.

7

Jumping for Distance
(Broad Jumping and Hop-Step-Jump)

Did you ever try leaping or jumping over a puddle of water or a small ditch? It's a lot of fun and you get a real sense of accomplishment after a good jump. But there are skills that you must learn in order to become a really good distance jumper.

The champion distance jumpers have speed, leg explosive power (spring in their legs), and body coordination. You will learn more about these requirements later in the chapter. First, let's find out where and when the jumping-for-distance events began.

History of Jumping for Distance

The *broad jump* was the only jumping event in the Ancient Olympic Games, and the Greeks used weights in their hands to help them get greater distance. These weights were called *"halteres."* They were made of metal or stone and weighed from two to ten pounds each.

The Greek broad jumpers would swing the weights forward and backward while in the air, to help propel arm and leg action for greater distance.

These weights were the origin or beginning of what are known today as "dumbbell" exercises. Up until 1850, the

British professionals used five-pound dumbbell weights in the standing and running broad jumps. They broke many records.

EARLY GREEK LANDING AREA. The ground in front of the takeoff was dug up and leveled to a certain distance. This "pit" or landing area was called the *"skamma,"* which means soft area.

The jumper's takeoff spot was marked by spears stuck in the ground.

BROAD JUMPING IN AMERICA. The broad jump first became an event of an American track and field program in 1868. It is believed that the first true American championship broad-jumping event took place in an amateur championship meet of 1876.

Some historians claim that George Washington and Abraham Lincoln were champions of their day and were said to have jumped more than twenty-two feet.

The *takeoff board* or "foul line" was first introduced for the broad-jumping event during the early American championship track and field meets.

Soon colleges began to offer the broad-jumping event in their championship track and field meets.

High schools introduced the broad-jump event around 1900.

OLYMPIC EVENT. The running broad jump in the first Modern Olympic Games in 1896 was won by Ellery Clark, an outstanding Harvard athlete. In the 1900 Olympics, the standing broad jump was won by Ray Ewry. As a young boy Ewry was an invalid and had almost died. His family doctor suggested he take up running and jumping exercises. He practiced constantly and worked tirelessly. He competed in the Olympics and won ten championships before he retired from active competition.

SAMPLE HAND WEIGHTS USED FOR JUMPING IN ANCIENT GREECE

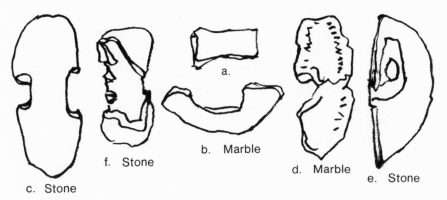

a.

f. Stone

b. Marble

c. Stone

d. Marble

e. Stone

Today the broad jump is better known throughout the world as the *long jump*.

Construction of Broad-jump Area

The following are regulations for constructing a championship jumping area. Remember, you do not need a championship construction area to practice the broad jump. Just check carefully to see that the area is safe. The running-broad-jump area can be divided into three parts: the runway, the takeoff board, and the landing area.

The *runway* is the running area between the takeoff board and the area where the broad jumper begins his run. There is no limit to the length of the runway, but it must not be less than 130-feet long. The runway areas can be of grass, cinders, or an artificial type of turf.

The *takeoff board* consist of a wooden board eight inches wide and at least four feet long. The takeoff board for high-school meets can be twenty-four inches wide and four feet long. The board must be thick enough so it can be fixed or fastened to the ground in such a way that it will not move when a jumper steps on it. The top side of the board must be level with the runway surface. The edge of the takeoff board nearest the landing area is known as the *scratch* or *foul line*.

The *landing area* is also known as the *landing pit*. This pit must be at least nine feet wide. The distance between the foul line and the nearest edge of the landing pit must be not less than three feet, three inches. The distance between the foul line and the farthest edge of the landing pit must be not less than twenty-nine feet, five inches. The sand in the landing area must be level with the takeoff board.

Don't forget to look for a safe place to practice. You do not need a large area. Check with your parents or teacher about a safe place to practice your jumps. Let's start with the standing broad jump.

Standing Broad Jump

The standing broad jump is a popular event in track and field meets for young boys and girls. You can practice the standing broad jump safely almost anywhere, indoors or outdoors.

The standing broad jump is usually divided into four parts: (1) the starting position, (2) the jump, (3) position in air, and (4) the landing.

THE STARTING POSITION. The jumper starts with both feet on the takeoff board or behind the takeoff line. The feet are about a shoulder-width apart. The arms are swung backward and forward, while the body is in a crouched position and the knees are bent.

Now, swing your arms backward and forward for a second time. Note the rocking motion of your arms and body. On the third backward and forward arm swing, you are ready for the jump.

THE JUMP. As your arms swing swiftly forward and upward on the third rocking motion, your body is actually leaning forward. Push off hard with your toes driving off the board. At the same time, swing forward and up with all the strength at your command. Keep your eyes focused beyond the point where you expect to land.

Position in Air. After the takeoff, bring your knees up close to your body. Keep your eyes forward. Swing your arms down while the body is leaning forward.

The Landing. Just before the feet land, your arms have reached a forward position to keep you from falling back. Your feet land with the knees and ankles relaxed to avoid jarring the body. You are now ready to fall lightly forward. Keep your balance, slightly forward, to prevent falling backward.

Jumping distance is measured from the takeoff line to the nearest mark on the surface caused by any part of the body. This means that if the jumper lands on his feet and then falls backward, the distance will be measured not from takeoff to his heel marks, but from takeoff to the nearest point on the ground touched by him.

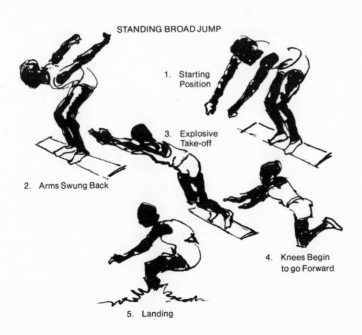

STANDING BROAD JUMP

1. Starting Position

2. Arms Swung Back

3. Explosive Take-off

4. Knees Begin to go Forward

5. Landing

Here is a test to see whether you have timing and explosive power in your leg muscles. It is one more part of the total Youth Physical Fitness Test prepared by the President's Council on Physical Fitness and Sports.

a. Take a position just behind the takeoff line, with your feet from six to ten inches apart. Be sure your stance is comfortable.

b. Bend your knees and swing your arms back and forth with an even motion.

c. Lean a trifle forward, swing your arms swiftly forward and upward, and take off from the balls of your feet with an explosive spring through the air.

Measure the distance from the takeoff line to the spot where your heels or any part of your body landed nearest to the takeoff line.

Repeat this exercise three times and measure each jump.

Write down the mark of your best jump in feet and inches for your score.

STANDING BROAD JUMP (BOYS)

Rating	Age— 10	11	12	13	14	15	16	17
				Feet–Inches				
Excellent	6–1	6–3	6–6	7–2	7–9	8–0	8–5	8–6
Presidential Award	5–8	5–10	6–2	6–9	7–3	7–6	7–11	8–1
Good	5–7	5–9	6–1	6–7	7–0	7–6	7–9	8–0
Satisfactory	5–2	5–4	5–8	6–0	6–7	6–0	7–4	7–6
Poor	4–10	5–0	5–4	5–7	6–1	6–6	6–11	7–0

Key: This jump is measured in feet and inches. The first number shows the feet and the second number shows the inches.

Example: 6-1 is six feet, one inch.

Note: If you are under ten years old, use the test as an exercise and *do not try* to see if you can keep up with older boys and girls.

STANDING BROAD JUMP (GIRLS)

Rating	Age— 10	11	12	13	14	15	16	17
					Feet–Inches			
Excellent	5–8	6–2	6–3	6–3	6–4	6–6	6–7	6–8
Presidential Award	5–4	5–8	5–9	5–10	6–0	6–1	6–2	6–2
Good	5–2	5–6	5–8	5–8	5–10	6–0	6–0	6–0
Satisfactory	4–10	5–0	5–2	5–3	5–5	5–6	5–6	5–7
Poor	4–5	4–8	4–9	4–10	5–0	5–1	5–2	5–2

Running Broad Jump (Long Jump)

Now let's see what skills are needed for the running broad jump.

The running broad jump is lots of fun. All you need is a soft and safe landing area or pit.

To learn and practice the long jump correctly, it is best to divide the jump into four parts: (1) the *run* or *approach,* (2) the *takeoff,* (3) the *flight,* (4) the *landing.*

THE RUN OR APPROACH. After many practice periods, each jumper decides what his best distance toward the takeoff board should be.

Make sure you don't take too long a run and tire just before you reach the takeoff board. But too short a run prevents you from picking up speed and height just before the jump. So practice and gauge your own distance.

Many jumpers put sticks or small flags as *markers* to one side of the runway during practice. These markers let you know exactly how many strides or steps you take between the start of your run and the one-foot takeoff from the board.

Let's pretend you chose a distance of about seventy feet for your run, and your left leg is the strong leg. One marker is placed at a distance of two running strides from the starting line. The second marker is located four strides from the first marker.

Now here is what you must do to make a good run for the jump:

1. Take a standing-start position with your *left* (*strong*) *foot* forward on the starting line.

2. Your second running stride or step reaches the first marker with the *left foot*.

3. Your next four strides reach the next marker also with the *left foot*.

4. Continue your run at full speed.

5. When you get within twenty-five to thirty feet of the takeoff board, you must relax and swing into a smooth running stride. *Do not* lessen your speed.

6. Look at the takeoff board from the corner of your eyes when about five strides away.

7. As you reach the takeoff board with the *left foot,* imagine getting yourself ready to jump high and far.

Note: If your right leg is the stronger, you start with the right foot and reach the markers and takeoff board with the right foot.

RUNNING BROAD JUMP

1. Take-off   2. "Knee-Tuck" Height

3. Landing with Arms Swung Back   4. Arms Swung Forward for Balance

THE TAKEOFF. Most broad jumpers will reduce their sprint speed on the last two or three strides before driving off the board. This is done for accuracy and to get more "spring" in the jump.

It is important to reach the markers properly and to spring from the takeoff board correctly, at the same time concentrating mind and body on the coming leap.

1. The left foot, pointed straight ahead, is swiftly planted on the takeoff board. The heel touches first. Then the ball of the foot touches, then the toe. This is a heel-ball-toe or rock-up-on-toes idea.

2. Keep your eyes upward and straight ahead.

3. The left leg begins to bend a little at the knee so it will be ready for a "spring or vaulting action."

4. The right leg is bent at the knee with toe pointing backward and slightly down.

5. The right arm is swung forward and slightly across the body, while the left arm is swung backward.

6. Your body weight begins to move forward, and your toes are about ready to leave the board.

7. Now, at this very moment, use all your energy for developing "explosive power" that will give you force for height and distance.

8. You do this by quickly straightening the left takeoff leg with a strong push-off with the toes.

9. The right leg is brought strongly forward and upward with knee pointed straight ahead.

You are now in the air or in flight.

THE FLIGHT. Once your toes leave the takeoff board, try to see how long you can stay or "sit-in-the-air." At the same time, you are preparing yourself for a good landing.

1. Once the right leg is swung forward, tuck the knee quickly under the chest.

1. Heel Hits Take-off Board
2. Ready for Take-off
3. Right Foot Steps Forward in Air
4. Right Foot Swings Back
5. Feet and Arms Forward
6. Landing
7. Arms Balance Forward

2. The left or takeoff leg quickly follows the right leg in a *"knee-tuck"* or *"sit-in-the-air"* position.

3. Both arms are now swung forward.

4. The body begins to lean forward at the height of your leap.

5. With a quick backward swing of both arms, and the legs pointing forward, you are ready for the landing.

Naturally this position of the body in flight after leaving the takeoff board is known as the *knee-tuck* or *sit-in-the-air* style. It is the easiest to learn. Another style that older champions use is called the *hitch-kick* or *stride-in-the-air* position.

After you take off with the left foot on the *hitch-kick* style, you quickly bring your right foot forward. Once you reach the highest point of your jump, the right leg is straightened, then powerfully kicked down and back, then forward and upward again. In other words, you take two steps in the air with your right leg.

Your left leg quickly follows with a single kick upward and forward. Both legs meet together in the air, ready for a smooth landing.

THE LANDING. The landing is made with the legs pointing forward as far as possible. At the same time you try to keep good balance to prevent falling backward.

1. Your feet are pointing upward and forward just before the landing.

2. As the heels first touch the jumping pit, both arms are brought forward with a swift motion to help pull your body weight forward over the toes.

3. Pull your head and shoulders forward and down to help raise your hips. This keeps you from falling backward.

4. The landing is made with feet slightly spread apart.

5. Relax the knees and ankles to help take away some of the shock on the feet when landing.

6. The force (momentum) of your jump will make your body pass over your feet on the landing.

Your *measurement for the jump* is made from the nearest mark in the landing pit to the edge of the takeoff board.

Hop-step-jump (Triple Jump)

The hop-step-jump, which is also known as the triple jump can be exciting. Youngsters are thrilled at the idea of an all-out sprint before taking a series of three leaps into the air for distance. They are easy to do, but take a lot of practice and study if you wish to perform well.

Some historians say that the early Greeks practiced a form of the triple jump, again using weights in their hands. But it was used little as an event in track and field programs.

The triple jump first became popular in America in an AAU program held in 1893. The event was included for the first time in the 1896 Olympics and won by James B. Connolly. He took two hops on one leg and a jump.

The Olympic programs in 1900 and 1904 also included the standing hop-step-jump event, won by the remarkable Ray Ewry. Some historians claim that Ewry won the event with three standing broad jumps in a row.

High schools began to introduce the event in their track and field programs as early as 1930. Today you will find the hop-step-jump event in most schools and playgrounds of America.

The runway and the landing pit for the broad jump are also used for the hop-step-jump event. The only difference is that the takeoff board is placed farther away from the landing pit so the jumpers can take the *hop* and *step* on flat ground, while the *jump* part allows them to land on the soft landing area.

RULES FOR THE TRIPLE JUMP. The athlete must make his first jump (*the hop*), by landing on the same foot from which he took off from the takeoff board.

His second jump (*the step*) must land him on the opposite foot.

The third *jump* is made with both feet landing just as in the regular running broad jump.

For example: If you decide to hit the takeoff board with the right foot, you must land on the *right foot* to complete your *hop*. The *step* is then made by landing on the *left foot,* and the *jump* is made by landing on both feet as in the broad jump.

APPROACH OR RUN BEFORE THE HOP. The run toward the takeoff board is similar to that used for the broad jump. Start your run anywhere from seventy feet to 120 feet, whichever is most comfortable to you.

Start your run with the strong foot forward. This will allow you to use the stronger jumping leg at the takeoff for the *hop* and the takeoff for the *step,* and then use the weaker leg for the *jump.*

If you plan to become a champion in this event, it is a good idea to strengthen both legs.

Now let's decide your right leg is the stronger and you are ready to make the hop.

HOW TO MAKE THE HOP. In making the hop, you try to get forward speed, keeping the body low.

As the right (strong) foot reaches the takeoff board, push off forward on the toes. Keep your hop low. Now drive the left leg forward. The right leg follows with the knee forward. Then suddenly straighten the whole right leg forward and land on the heel or ball of the foot. Your body is in an upright position.

MAKING THE STEP. Now push off from the toes of your right foot. Continue forward and slightly upward with a thrust or stride with the left foot. Your body is leaning just a bit forward.

The left foot *step* lands on the heel first, then on the ball and toes. With a rocking heel-ball-toe action you are ready for the jump.

THE JUMP. Push off hard with the left foot and land on both feet in the pit.

The jump is made by using the same skills used for the running broad jump. Try to get height and distance.

Most young athletes will discover that the hop gives

them the longest distance of their three units of the triple jump. The jump portion usually gives the next best distance, and the step gives the shortest length of the total triple-jump distance.

THE STANDING HOP-STEP-JUMP. This competition is fun to try. Place the foot of your stronger leg on the take-off board or behind the starting line. Lift the other foot off the ground just a bit.

Now swing the arms forward and backward a few times. Then give an explosive push-off with your leg for the hop. The step and jump skills are similar to those used in the running hop-step-jump.

Get out and practice. You will find joy and a feeling of success after training for these skills.

Hints

1. Try to find a soft outdoor landing area for the running-broad-jump and hop-step-jump events.

2. If an official landing pit is not available, use mats for either indoor or outdoor events.

3. Take part in warm-up exercises before competing.

Drills and Exercises

1. Choose a partner and practice the standing broad jump. Check one another for distance and form.

2. From a standing-broad-jump position, jump forward three times without stopping. Challenge a friend and see who reaches the farthest distance for three straight jumps.

3. Try hopping up and down twelve times on one foot. Change and hop on the other foot. Repeat three times on each foot.

4. Hop forward six times on one foot; then on the other

foot six times. Now hop only three times on one foot, but go for distance. Can you beat your old record? Or a friend?

5. Practice the "hop and step" together. Then try the "step and jump" together. Challenge a friend to see who can go the farthest distance.

6. Work on the distance of your run toward the takeoff board. Are you reaching the board or line with the strong leg?

7. Work for extra height on the takeoff for the broad jump. Have a friend hold a pole or branch across the jumping pit, with an old hat or piece of cloth tied to the pole. See if you can touch the hat or cloth with your head after the jump.

8. Other good leg exercises are:
    a. Stepping up and down on an old stool, chair, bench, etc.
    b. Climbing stairs.
    c. Walking and jogging uphill.
    d. Heel-raising with toes over a small block of wood.
    e. Lifting a bundle of newspapers or magazines resting on top of one of your thighs.

8

Jumping for Height
(High Jumping and Pole Vaulting)

The two events in sports that test a man's skill in propelling himself into the air are the running high jump and the pole vault. In the high jump the athlete uses muscles in his legs to spring into the air. In the pole vault he has a pole to help him get into the air.

How did these two events become a part of the track and field program? Let's take the *high jump* first.

History of High Jumping

The Irish included the high jump in the program of their ancient Tailtean Games over 2,500 years ago. During the Middle Ages, at village fairs and before royalty, traveling acrobats performed such feats as aerial somersaults, wall jumping, and leaping over the heads of their partners.

At a track and field meet between Oxford and Cambridge Universities in 1864 the high jump was included as a competitive event. Oxford and Cambridge were the first universities to do this.

HIGH JUMPING IN AMERICA. Many writers believe that high-jumping competition in America was first introduced as an event of a track and field program in 1868. The amateur athletic organizations began to place the high jump in their program in 1876.

An American broke the world record for the high jump in 1887, using what is known as the old scissors-style jump. This is clearing the bar in a sitting kind of position. In 1895, another American broke the world record using the scissors jump. He went over the bar one foot at a time, but flattened his body out, his back toward the ground, as he cleared the bar. This skill soon became known as the *Eastern-style* jump, because the jumper was from the Eastern part of the United States.

The first Modern Olympic Games in 1896 included the high-jump event in the program. Shortly after 1896, colleges and schools began to include the high jump as a track and field event. High jumping for girls was first included in the 1928 Olympic games.

In 1910, a Stanford University jumper began to break records in the high jump. People soon began to call his style of high jumping the *Western-roll style,* because he was from the West. In this style, the jumper ran toward the bar from a forty-five-degree angle and from the opposite side of the bar than that approached for the Eastern style.

In 1930, still another revolutionary style of high jumping was introduced. This was known as the *straddle style* or "belly roll." Here the jumper straddles the bar one leg at a time, with his belly facing the bar as he continues to complete his jump.

One of the biggest surprises in the world of sports took place at the 1968 Olympics in Mexico City. Dick Fosbury, a great jumper from Oregon State University, ran toward the crossbar. He took off with an explosive push forward and upward, and then suddenly turned his back to the bar as his head, shoulders, back, and legs cleared it, in that order, and he won the Olympic championship. This style of high jumping was soon called the *Fosbury-flop* because he "flopped" on his back after clearing the bar. Of course this style of jumping is not for youngsters unless it is done only when a thick foam mattress is used as the landing pit. A teacher must be available to check for safety.

What Style Is Best?

Teachers and coaches have not yet found the *best* technique to use for high jumping. But most agree that the "scissors" style is the easiest and most natural for a youngster to learn. The "Eastern" style is not as good as the "Western" and "straddle" styles to achieve or gain the most height. The "straddle" and "Fosbury-Flop" are more difficult to learn, but they are the most popular styles among the great high jumpers of the world today.

You will first learn and study the "scissors" style. In this chapter, you will also be shown how to perform the "Western" and "straddle" styles. However, wait until you grow a little stronger, or have a teacher to help you, before spending a lot of time on these more difficult skills.

Equipment for High Jump

The outdoor high-jump runway or approach is usually about fifty feet in length from the start of the run to the crossbar. The ground should be level. Indoor runways are sometimes shorter.

The upright pole standards are two inches square and are fastened on a heavy base that rests on the ground. The two uprights can be of any height, depending on the competition. The standards are marked by feet and inches with holes drilled at every inch to allow the small "pegs" to fit. Adjustable clamps around each upright standard pole are often used in place of holes for the pegs. The crossbar is made of wood or metal and rests on top of the pegs.

Official regulations for the high-jump landing area or pit state it should be sixteen feet wide and twelve feet long. It is recommended that the pit be covered about twenty-four to thirty-six inches deep with wood shavings, sawdust, or foam-rubber matting.

The shoes for high jumping are similar to those for track, but most jumpers wear a heel cup inside their take-off-foot shoe. Some jumpers are known to wear a different type of shoe on each foot, and a few don't wear any shoe on the foot that goes over the crossbar first.

Go for "Spring" Action

To be successful in the running high jump, you must develop strong *"spring"* action or *"explosive power"* in your legs. Speed is not most important. You must use all your energy to propel yourself high into the air and over the bar.

If you work hard and develop a good spring action, time your run properly, and get good body coordination, you will experience lots of fun and success in high jumping.

Each jumper must decide from practice and experience the proper distance to the crossbar. Each jumper, also, decides on the angle of approach or run toward the crossbar and the foot that will be used for the upward takeoff jump.

Let's find out all about these skills—and more.

The Scissors High Jump

The scissors-style high jump can be divided into three parts. The *approach* or *run,* the *takeoff,* and the *landing.*

THE APPROACH OR RUN. This is what you do if you are a right-footed kicker, which means your left leg is the strong takeoff leg:

1. Take a running-start position about seven strides (steps) away from the right side of the crossbar.

2. You are now at about a fifteen to thirty-degree angle to the bar, so you will approach it from the right side.

3. Lean forward, let your arms hang loosely in front of you. Study the path of your approach run, as well as to the bar. Now, relax and concentrate on your jump for a few seconds.

4. Start your approach to the bar with your left (strong) foot. Take your first three steps rather slowly.

5. Take the next four steps faster and longer.

6. Plant your last step with the left (strong) foot one arm's length from the bar. Your right side is now facing the bar.

THE TAKEOFF. The takeoff is made on the last, left-foot step which is farthest from the crossbar.

1. Rock up on the ball of the takeoff foot with a spring-like push upward.

2. Quickly kick up your right (inside) leg.

3. At the same time swing your arms up. This gives you upward motion.

4. Pretend you are reaching for all the height you can.

5. The right (inside) leg continues over the bar, followed swiftly by the left (outside) leg in an upward scissors action.

6. Keep the left (outside) leg as straight as possible to prevent hitting the bar with your heel. You are now practically in a sitting position in the air over the bar.

THE LANDING. As you clear the crossbar, straighten your body, while leaning slightly forward. Try to relax and land on the right leg first, quickly followed by the left. Keep your arms forward and knees bent to break the force of the landing.

After you have learned how to perform the scissors jump well, you may begin to practice the Western jump.

A right-footed kicker will run for the crossbar from the left side, when using the Western-style jump. (Left-footed kickers run for the bar from the right side.)

If you take an odd number of steps (seven or nine) toward the bar, you must start your run with the left foot. If you take an even number of steps (eight or ten), you start your run with the right foot. This will let you make the takeoff push over the bar with your strong left leg.

THE APPROACH. You decide to take nine strides (steps) to start your approach for the bar. You face the bar from about a forty-five-degree angle. Start your first three steps slowly and pick up speed for the remaining steps.

Plant your last step with the strong (left) foot about one arm's length from the bar. Your left side is facing the bar.

THE WESTERN STYLE JUMP

1. After Take-off

2. Clearing the Bar

3. Landing

THE TAKEOFF. To make a good explosive and upward takeoff, the last step must be planted in the direction of your run (not pointed toward the bar).

Land on your heel, as your body leans backward. Now the foot rolls into a "heel-ball-toes" rocking action, ready for the takeoff. The speedy forward motion of the body passes over and past the toes, ready for a "spring" action.

The outside (right) leg begins its upward kick with a slightly bent knee, alongside (parallel to) the bar.

Now, with your knee slightly bent, take an explosive spring upward off your left foot. Both arms swing swiftly upward and forward. The outside (right) leg begins to straighten out alongside and over the bar. Your eyes are looking directly over the bar.

The knee of your takeoff leg is quickly drawn up toward your chin, directly under your top right leg. You are now in what is known as a *Western lay-out position* over the bar. It looks just as if you are lying over the bar on your right side.

From this position, begin to turn your body toward the landing pit. Straighten out your head and body as your left arm, shoulder, and hip pass over the bar. Keep your eyes looking down toward the pit.

THE LANDING. The landing is made on both hands and left (takeoff) foot. To absorb the shock of your landing, bend your left knee and both elbows.

The Straddle-style Jump

Make certain you master the skills of the scissors and Western-style jumps before you work on the straddle form.

THE APPROACH. The approach or run before the take-off is practically the same as for the Western style. The main difference is that you would start your run from a twenty to thirty-degree angle from the crossbar. This is closer to the bar than for the Western style.

Don't forget to decide on the number of strides so you will take off from your stronger leg. Let's see how you would make the jump with a left foot takeoff.

THE TAKEOFF. This is made with the foot (left) closest to the bar. The outside (right) leg is kicked swiftly upward and alongside the bar, and *not over the center of the bar*.

The arms swing upward as the body is turning toward the bar. As you reach the very top of your jump, the right leg, chest, and head are directly over the bar.

In other words, you are in a straddle or "belly" position facing the bar. To continue rolling over the bar, swing your right arm back and upward. Your hips should now continue to roll over the bar, providing a good lift to your left leg as your toes turn upward to clear the bar.

On this jump, keep your hands at your sides while clearing the bar.

2. Straddle over Bar

3. Ready for Landing

STRADDLE STYLE JUMP

4. Landing

1. After Take-off

THE LANDING. You land on the right hand and right foot, with a roll over the right shoulder. Some jumpers land on both hands and the right foot before continuing to roll.

These three styles of jumping certainly look like a lot of work, but remember what you were told earlier.

Start your training by devoting your time to learning the scissors-jump skills first. You will soon discover you can make more jumps easily, and it's more fun, too. You will also find out that the better you know the scissors skills, the easier the more-advanced jumps will be later.

The Pole Vault

The pole vault is one of the most difficult skills to learn, but it is also one of the most spectacular of all track events. It is a great thrill to soar over the crossbar, high in the air, with the use of a pole.

There are few soft places on which to do pole vaulting, and it is also very important that the right equipment be used to eliminate any possibility of injury.

For these reasons, do not spend a lot of time practicing for this event unless you have a teacher or parent helping you. As you grow older, though, you will probably begin to enjoy learning these skills.

However, it is interesting to know where the pole vault originated. How did it become an event in the modern track and field programs, and what equipment and skills are used by the champions today?

History of the Pole Vault

There is no recorded history that the pole vault was used for competition in the Ancient Olympic Games. Most historians believe that primitive men used the skills of jumping with a pole as a wartime exercise. They needed this skill to jump over streams and gullies to escape their enemies or wild beasts.

Some historians claim that the Irish competed in an event called "pole jumping" in the Ancient Tailtean Games of Ireland. These people also used a pole to clear water hazards, gullies, ditches, and bogs found in the marshy land along the North Sea.

In these early years, pole jumping was a contest or skill for distance rather than height.

Pole-vaulting competition began in England and Germany about the year 1800. In Germany it was practiced at first as a gymnasium sport for distance. Then, in about 1850, it became a contest for height. It is believed that in 1850 the English originated the idea of a contest, using a pole and vaulting for height. The English at this time used long, heavy poles, usually of ash or hickory, with a tripod or triangular piece of iron at the lower end of the pole. This helped to keep the pole from sliding when it was placed on the ground.

The first time that pole-vaulting competition for height took place in America was in a track meet in 1877. The American jumpers eagerly responded to the new event and soon set new pole-vaulting records.

The English vaulters also developed new skills. They would use the pole to vault and then pull themselves over the crossbar by climbing up the pole with their hands. These English jumpers were called "pole climbers."

American rules forbid this form of jumping. The World Olympic Game Rules Committee also made it illegal in 1890. Rules now began to be written so that all competitors from all nations would know the exact skills that must be mastered for world competition.

The first poles used for actual competition were made of ash, spruce, or hickory wood. Next came the bamboo poles with a spiked edge at the bottom. The iron-spiked edge was soon replaced with a mushroom-shaped plug to help keep the poles from slipping on the ground during the jump. Steel tips and plugs were eliminated from the poles when the rules permitted takeoff holes in the ground to prevent the poles from slipping.

A wooden vaulting box was first used in the 1924 Olympics. This box was secured to the ground so jumpers could plant their poles into the vaulting box while running at top speed. These vaulting boxes soon led to the use of new and improved poles. Many vaulters began to use steel and aluminum poles, and new records were set. Today the vaulting boxes are made out of durable aluminum or steel.

The biggest improvement in pole vaulting took place in 1962 when the fiberglass poles were made legal by the International Amateur Athletic Federation. The pole usually has a rubber plug on the bottom and a cork on the top end.

To help the vaulter, a (black-and-white painted) *striped crossbar* was first introduced in 1920. Then the runway area leading to the vaulting box was improved with smooth and fast artificial materials. Instead of wood shavings, sawdust, or sand in the landing pit, *foam rubber* was used to eliminate some of the shock the jumpers feel when landing. The pole-vault standards are similar to the high-jump standards. The uprights are made of wood, aluminum, plastic, or steel. The landing pit area should be at least sixteen feet wide and twelve feet long. The upright standards are placed twelve feet apart.

Qualifications for Championship Pole Vaulting

The first qualification is a doctor's examination to find out if the pole vaulter is physically and mentally healthy. Although any boy can take part and have fun, he must concentrate on a training program that will develop skills necessary for competitive pole vaulting.

AGE. There is no specific age for learning pole-vaulting skills. If you plan to compete, you should have the advice of a teacher or parent. Otherwise, build up and develop your skills, but wait until you are older and stronger before you begin to vault in actual competition. If your school has a track coach, report to him and learn all you can.

HEIGHT. Most experts claim that taller boys usually do better than shorter boys in the pole vault. But remember, with hard work and courage smaller athletes can break records—as has been proved.

HEART AND BREATHING ENDURANCE. In regular competition, the pole-vault contest often lasts a long time. The jumpers take many runs at different heights. This means your heart and breathing must be strong and your mind alert to last throughout the competition.

SPEED. The pole vaulter must have just enough speed to help lift his body to the upright position of the pole. However, the vaulter does not have to run at a sprinter's speed to be successful.

EXPLOSIVE LEG POWER. The vaulter uses explosive leg power or "spring" from the takeoff leg to help him and the pole rocket forward and upward.

ARMS AND SHOULDER STRENGTH AND ENDURANCE. The arms and shoulder muscles help the vaulter to pull himself up the pole on the takeoff and to push up and away on the pole upon reaching the highest point of the vault to go over the bar.

BODY COORDINATION. To coordinate these complicated actions, the vaulter must achieve perfect physical conditioning and coordination. He must utilize all the different body skills and movements together, at the right time, to make a successful vault.

CONFIDENCE IN LANDING. The vaulter must not worry about landing from a great height, or the strength of his pole. He should concentrate on the one important object of his training—to clear the crossbar.

Now let's see how the pole vaulter starts and finishes a jump.

Pole-vault Action

The total action of a pole vaulter from start to finish involves many different skills. Only when they are all put together does the vaulter achieve success. These are some of the main skills or parts that make up the total jump.

THE GRIP. The right-handed vaulter holds the pole at the top end with the right-hand palm underneath the pole. The left hand grasps the pole with the palm down, from twenty-four to thirty-six inches in front of the right hand.

THE POLE CARRY. The front tip of the pole should be carried about head high, pointing straight ahead. The right arm is straightened back and down. The left arm is directly across the body at about waist height. Some vaulters prefer to carry the pole slightly turned across the body at the beginning of the run.

THE RUN. Vaulters pace off a run anywhere from ninety to 150 feet before the takeoff jump. The speed of the run depends on the ability of the athlete. The important point is to attain your greatest speed with the takeoff on the strong foot. Most vaulters begin the run slowly and pick up speed just before the jump. Markers on the side of the runway help to guide the vaulter's run.

THE HAND SHIFT. The hand shift takes place just as you begin to lower the tip of the pole into the V-shaped vaulting box. The right hand is swung forward and upward past the head, and the left hand is shifted up to the right until both hands are fully extended. The left-hand grip slides upward to about four inches from the right-hand grip. Many vaulters do not use a handshift.

POLE PLANT INTO VAULTING BOX. There are two methods of placing the pole into the vaulting box: the *overhand plant* and the *underhand plant*. The underhand type is the most popular. This is the most natural style of dropping the pole into the box. The right hand is brought forward past the body. The pole continues to move forward and upward toward the box until the pole and arms are over the athlete's head. It is important to keep a tight grip on the pole when it hits the back end of the box.

THE TAKEOFF. The takeoff is made on the left (strong) leg for a good spring action. Your feet leave the ground and your hips begin to swing forward and upward with the pole. The body should hang from the extended arms and swing forward and upward like a pendulum.

THE PULL-UP. As the vaulter's upward-forward swing ends, he must pull up, using his arms on the pole. It takes timing to pull up swiftly just as the body reaches the highest swing level. The pole is now in an almost vertical position near the crossbar. The vaulter's body begins to turn, facing the runway with hips near the pole.

THE PUSH-UP. The vaulter continues to turn his chest toward the runway and over the bar. The arms make a hard pushing action upward to get the legs up and over the bar. To clear the bar, the vaulter first releases the left hand. Then, with a strong push-up-and-away movement with the right arm, he releases the pole and is over the bar. The pole is pushed away from hitting the crossbar.

THE LANDING. After clearing the bar, the vaulter should fall completely relaxed, with the body extended to reduce the shock of the fall.

Hints

1. Follow all safety rules before practicing the different jumps.

2. Start your practice by learning the scissors jump first.

3. Have an adult help you when trying the Western, Fosbury-flop, or straddle styles.

4. Do not try actual pole-vault jumping without adult help.

Drills

1. Work on the drills and exercises listed in Chapter Seven.

2. Do high-step kicking for spring in your legs.
   a. Put one hand straight out in front of you with palm down. Try kicking your hand with the right foot, left foot. Repeat ten times.
   b. Tie two- to five-pound weights (sandbags, magazines, stones) around an ankle or foot. Now try kicking upward six times. Repeat with weight on opposite foot.

3. For explosive leg jump and reach, put up a long piece of blank wrapping paper or a smooth piece of cardboard against a wall. With your toes against the wall and a piece of chalk in your right hand, stretch as high as you can. Make a small chalk mark. Now relax and move several inches from the wall. Jump up with a good leg spring and make another chalk mark. Measure the distance between the two markers. Try with chalk in the left hand. Challenge a partner.

9

The Great Throwing Events
(Shot-Put, Discus, Javelin, Hammer, Weight, Baseball and Basketball Throws)

Most young people can participate safely in the shot-put, but the discus, javelin, hammer, and weight throws are not recommended until you grow older and stronger. These events are safe only when the equipment is used correctly and a coach is with you. However, the baseball and basketball throws for distance are often included in track and field programs for boys and girls.

The Shot-put

Historians do not agree on exactly where the shot-put event originated. Some writers trace its beginnings back 2,500 years to people called the "Celts" who settled in Scotland and Ireland. These ancient Scots and Irish took part in a contest called "putting the stone," which weighed about fourteen pounds. The event was included in the Irish Tailtean Games.

Around the year 1540, a contest called "weight putting" was popular in England. King Henry VIII, a fine competitor himself, halted the event because it threatened to replace archery, which was a skill needed in war.

The great Scottish poet, Sir Walter Scott, who died in 1832, wrote that "putting the stone" was an important contest in the National Scottish Games.

There are games of distance throws today in many countries, and the participants use whatever object is plentiful. In Northern Afghanistan in Asia, where melons are plentiful, children and young adults compete in a melon throw for distance. The poorer villagers eat the remains after the contest is concluded.

The first iron shot-puts were shaped like a block. Being made of metal, they were heavy and awkward to throw. Later they were made into ball-shaped missiles.

A RUNNING THROW. The early rules allowed the athlete to run with the iron ball in his hand up to a foul line and throw the ball for distance. After the iron ball was released, the shot-putter was allowed to step past the foul line.

FIRST SHOT-PUT CIRCLE. In 1875, a seven-foot circle was drawn, and the athlete had to make his "push" or "put" (not a throw) from within the circle.

The first shot-putting events in American championship meets took place in 1876.

The sixteen-pound shot-put became a regular event of the Olympic games in 1896. The seven-foot *circular platform* was first used in the 1904 Olympics. The shot-put event for women was first held in the 1948 Olympic games. Women were allowed to use an eight-pound, thirteen-ounce shot made of iron or brass.

Today shot-put competition is a popular track and field event in colleges, schools, playgrounds, parks, and clubs.

Shot-put Equipment

THE SHOT. The weight for the shot you will use depends on the kind of competition. For world and college competition, the weight of the shot is sixteen pounds for men; eight pounds, thirteen ounces for women. High-school boys use the eight-pound shot. High-school girls also use an eight-pound shot. Youngsters may use a shot weighing anywhere from four, six, or eight pounds, depending on their age, weight, and experience.

The outdoor shots are made of steel or brass. The indoor shots are made of plastic or leather covering with lead weights inside.

SHOT-CIRCLE PLATFORMS. In championship meets, a platform of steel sheets, wood, or permanent cement is used. The platforms are marked with a seven-foot circle. The athlete must start and finish his push of the shot within the circle. For other meets, a line two inches wide may be used when a platform and two-inch metal band circle is not available.

A shot-put *toe board* is tightly fastened to form a true arc four feet in front of the seven-foot circle. The rest of the toe board is four inches high and four and one-half inches wide. Most toe boards are made of layers of wood or aluminum. The toe board allows the athlete to step against the board with great force and helps to prevent him from "stepping over" the line, thereby committing a foul.

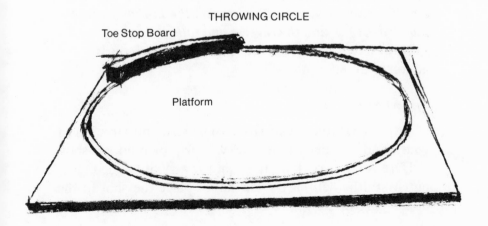

THROWING CIRCLE

Toe Stop Board

Platform

There are rules that govern the competitor in all throwing events. The rules for the shot-put are:

1. The *push* or *put* must start from a stationary position in the circle.
2. The competitor cannot leave the circle until the shot hits the ground.
3. You are allowed to touch the inside of the toe board, but not on top, for that is a foul.
4. The shot must land inside the specific marked area or boundary to be fair.
5. The shot must be pushed or putted with one hand from the shoulder near the chin.
6. The distance of the *put* is measured from inside front-center of the circle to nearest mark on the ground made by the shot.

Qualifications

Shot-putters must have good strength in the fingers, hand, wrist, arm, shoulder, and leg. A shot-putter develops explosive arm power and speed in his pushing arm. He also needs good leg balance and outstanding body coordination.

The shot-put can be divided into different parts. They are *the grasp of the shot, the stance, the hop or glide, the put or delivery,* and *the reverse and follow-through.*

Now let's see how these skills are used during the action of the shot-put.

Shot-put Action

THE GRASP OR HAND HOLD. The size and strength of your hand will determine how you grip or hold the shot.

Here is how you hold the shot for a right-handed shot-put. With the help of the left hand, place the shot in the upper part of the palm of the right hand. Most of the

Full Hand Grip (Back View)

weight of the ball is on the base of the middle three fingers. Keep your fingers spread equally behind the shot, with the thumb to the side for balance.

Shift the shot to a position slightly above and directly in front of the shoulder, and rest it below the ear and jaw. Now, relax your wrist by allowing the weight of the shot to rest on your hand. The right elbow is level with your shoulder.

THE STANCE. Take a stance just inside the rear of the circle, with the right foot pointed toward the side. Keep most of your weight on the right foot. The toe of the left foot is a few inches behind and to the left of the heel of the right foot. Now lean your body weight over the right leg. Raise the left leg upward and forward, pointing toward the front of the circle. Your eyes are looking ahead. The left arm is in front of the body at chest height. You are now ready to move forward.

THE HOP OR GLIDE. The hop is sometimes indeed a hop. Sometimes it is a hop that slides into a glide. Hop with the right foot, and keep the hop very low. Barely touch the ground with the toe of the left foot for balance. Now get ready! Hop with the right foot, then lift the left foot up and forward again. Start to lean forward with the left hip and begin to make a powerful drive, starting off the right foot. The left leg shifts toward the toe board. Keep body low.

SHOT PUTTER IN ACTION

1. Stance

2. Ready for Hop or Glide

3. Completed Hop Ready for Put

4. The Put

5. Follow-through

Now, swiftly take one glide or hop straight forward across the center of the circle by straightening your right leg for additional force. Your body is slightly erect.

THE PUT OR DELIVERY. At the same time, start pushing the shot from the entire right side of your body. Keep driving off the right foot.

Just as you release the shot, step down on the right foot. At this very instant you push upward with all the strength in your right arm. For added power, use your wrist and fingers. Your weight is now shifted to the left foot, which is forward.

THE REVERSE AND FOLLOW-THROUGH. Once the shot has left the hand, make a quick reverse shift with your feet. Twist to the left on your right foot, which will bring it to the toe board. The left foot is now in back. This action stops you from falling past the toe board and committing a foul.

All this action seems complex and difficult, but *take your time*. Practice each movement a little at a time. You will soon find out that the various complex moves do become easier. It's fun trying to see how far you can "put that shot."

The Discus Throw

A discus thrower in action is often said to make one of the most beautiful sights in sports. In the early Olympic games, the discus was thrown from an elevated pedestal or platform. This limited the athlete's freedom to throw for distance. A free-style throwing action was introduced in the first Modern Olympic Games in 1896. Each competitor was asked to throw from a seven-foot circle on the ground.

DISCUS GRIPS

1. Grip for Small Hands

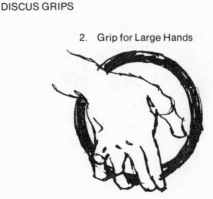

2. Grip for Large Hands

The discus-throwing event for women was first introduced in the program of the 1928 Olympics.

The discus became a regular event in American meets when it was put on the Amateur Athletic Union program in 1897.

In 1910, the International Amateur Athletic Federation adopted a *discus circle* measuring eight feet, two and one-half inches. This measurement is now used today in schools, colleges, and world competition.

DISCUS WEIGHT AND MEASUREMENT. For men, the discus must weigh not less than four pounds, six and four-tenths ounces. The size of the discus must not be less than eight and five-eighths inches round.

For high-school boys, the discus weight must not be less than three pounds, nine ounces. The size must not be less than eight and one-fourth inches round.

The discus weight must not be less than two pounds, three and one-fourth ounces for high-school and college girls and women. The size must not be less than seven and three thirty-seconds inches round.

The discus is thickest in the center (an inch and three-quarters), from where it starts to thin gradually to its edges. This is true of every discus, regardless of its weight.

THE DISCUS THROW

2. Completing Second Turn on Spin   3. Ready for Throw   4. Follow-through

1. Starting Stance

The discus is made of wood, steel, brass, bronze, aluminum, or rubber. The discus platform circles are made of wood, steel, or aluminum.

DISCUS THROWER IN ACTION. The athlete must start and end his throw in the circle. He holds the flatlike discus in the palm of his throwing hand. The ends of his four fingers curl around the edges of the discus. The thumb rests on side and back for control. The thrower bends one knee slightly, then swiftly begins to pivot his body. He makes a complete turn to gain speed and explosive power. At the end of a second turn, the athlete *hurls* the discus upward and forward, and follows through as his fingers spin the discus in a flat position into the air.

The Javelin Throw

The spear was used for war and hunting as far back as historians can trace. Spear and javelin throwing were taught to all youngsters in ancient times.

Today in some of the tribes of Netherlands New Guinea, the children are taught how to throw a spear right after they have learned to walk, and are soon skilled in a game they call "kill-the-hoop." The children "kill" a bouncing hoop by flinging their three-foot wooden spears through it. For them it is a skill they need for survival, just as much today as in ancient times. Many adult Eskimos play a dangerous game with spears to test and sharpen their throwing skills. The players wear heavy gloves and jab their harpoons at a hanging target that is full of holes. The first Eskimo to spear one of the drilled holes is the winner, and is thereafter considered by the rest of the tribe a good hunter and provider.

The javelin competition for men was not included in the Modern Olympic Games until 1906. The event for women was first introduced in the 1932 Olympics. However, the first javelin-throw competition in America took place in an Amateur Athletic Union program in 1909.

Not many high schools today sponsor the javelin throw. They must have strict safety rules if they do.

JAVELIN WEIGHT AND MEASUREMENT. For men, the javelin must not weigh less than one pound, twelve and one-quarter ounces. The length must not be less than eight feet, six and three-fourths inches. The center—thickest portion—of the javelin must not be more than one inch round. The javelin is round, but becomes gradually thinner as its rear and front portions are reached. The cord must not be less than six inches long.

For women, the javelin must not weigh less than one pound, five and two-tenths ounces. The length must not be less than seven feet, two and one-quarter inches. The cord grip at the center must be five and seven-eighths inches long.

The javelin is made of metal or solid wood with a metal head at the front tip and a hand grip, made of fine cord, at the center.

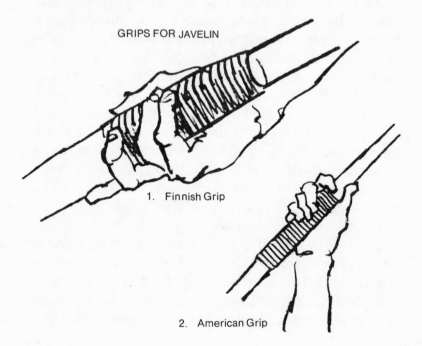

GRIPS FOR JAVELIN

1. Finnish Grip

2. American Grip

1. Over Shoulder Carry

2. Last Step Before Throw

3. Ready for Throw

4. Follow-through

THE JAVELIN THROWER IN ACTION. The thrower starts his run on a marked runway, facing the throwing area. He grasps the javelin on the cord grip, and holds and carries it in his favorite position. He runs toward the foul line, increasing his speed. The moment he reaches top speed, he brings the javelin back and hurls it upward and forward—just before reaching the foul line. The javelin must fall within the marked area with the front tip striking the ground first.

Most historians claim that a form of today's hammer throwing first began with the Celts over 2,500 years ago.

This event got its name because many years ago contestants used a "sledge hammer" for distance throwing. The competition was very popular with the nobility. There is a drawing of King Henry VIII of England, dated about 1535, showing him throwing a sledge hammer to demonstrate his physical skill to the people.

Scotland and Ireland made the hammer throw popular. The Irish-Americans were the main competitors and record-holders when the event was sponsored in the early American Championship Meets.

In 1887, the rules stated that the hammer would be round, of iron or brass, with a chain or steel cable four feet long connected to a handle. The hammer throw was first included in the 1900 Olympic games. In 1908, international rules were adopted, with a seven-foot circle in which to begin and end the throw.

HAMMER WEIGHT AND MEASUREMENT. The "ball" portion of the hammer is four to four and one-half inches round, weighing sixteen pounds. For high-school competition, the weight is twelve pounds. The ball is made of metal and may be filled with lead. The ball is connected to a single length of steel wire four feet long and not less than one-eighth of an inch thick. This wire is also known as the *handle* part of the hammer. The other end is connected to a grip made of metal. The seven-foot circle is made of steel, cement, or wood, but smooth turf is often used. A competitor may wear light gloves to protect his hands.

HAMMER THROWER IN ACTION. The thrower takes a firm two-handed grip on the hammer, stands with his feet about a shoulder-width apart, and places himself at the

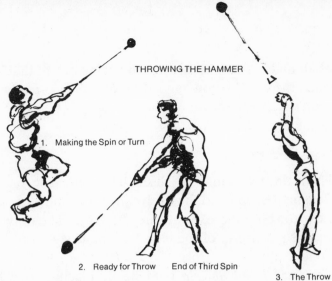

THROWING THE HAMMER

1. Making the Spin or Turn

2. Ready for Throw   End of Third Spin

3. The Throw

rear of the circle, with his back facing the throwing area. He then lifts the hammer and begins to turn or swing it around and over his head until he picks up his full swinging speed. Then he takes the first of three required spins in the circle. To gain speed, the thrower spins on his left foot. At the end of the third spin, the athlete releases the hammer upward and outward in the direction of the throwing area.

THE THIRTY-FIVE-POUND WEIGHT THROW. This event is not sponsored as often as the hammer throw. The rules are nearly the same. The only difference is that the "ball" weighs thirty-five pounds and is connected to a large-size steel grip, with no length of steel wire. The thrower spins and whirls the large weight for distance.

Baseball and Basketball Throws for Distance

Throwing the baseball and basketball for distance is included in many track and field meets throughout the country. Elementary schools, playgrounds, parks, high schools, and colleges sponsor these events in their programs.

Many of the same skills needed for the shot-put, javelin, and discus throws are also developed and used in the baseball and basketball throws. So it's important that you practice these skills now, and then you will be ready for the other events later.

The Baseball Throw

There are two kinds of baseball throws. The regular big-league baseball and the twelve-inch softball. The skills you use for both these events are the same. The only difference is in the grip of the ball. Let's start right now and begin to throw.

The *hard baseball grip* is made by placing your first two fingers on top and across the widest seam of the ball. Place your third and fourth fingers on the lower side of the ball. Keep your thumb on the bottom for control. Grip the ball firmly. The *softball grip* is made with three fingers spread evenly on top and across the ball. Your fourth finger is spread to the lower side of the ball, with the thumb on the bottom of the ball for control.

MAKING THE THROW. Mark a throwing or foul line on the ground. Take an outfielder's position about six to ten feet behind the throw line. Grip the ball and get set for

BASEBALL THROW FOR DISTANCE

1. Weight on Back Foot
2. Ready for Last Step
3. Ready for Throw
4. Follow-through

a long-distance overhead throw. Start moving forward with short sliding steps. Your throwing arm begins to wind up just before your last hop or step. The body weight shifts to the back foot. The front arm is held forward and points upward. Now, at the same time, swiftly bring your forward foot up and forward, and throw the ball upward and forward with all your strength. In other words, as the throw is made, the weight of your body is shifted over the front foot so that your entire body is behind the throw. Make a smooth follow-through by quickly bringing the rear foot forward for control.

That is all there is to it. Practice and concentrate on throwing form regularly if you wish to improve your distance.

Your Softball Throwing Test

This is a test to see whether you have coordination, timing, and explosive power in the shoulder and arm muscles of your throwing arm. It is one more part of the total Youth Physical Fitness Test prepared by the President's Council on Physical Fitness and Sports.

You can take this test on an open field, playground, football or baseball field. Use a twelve-inch softball. Mark a throwing-starting line. Have a partner measure the throw with a tape measure.

a. Take an outfielder's throwing position about six to ten feet behind the throwing line.

b. Start your wind-up and begin moving forward at the same time.

c. Get as close as possible to the starting line and throw the ball overhand as far as you can.

Do not step over the throwing line or it will be a foul. Your partner will place a stake to mark the spot where the ball hit the ground. You are allowed to have three tries, and the best one is set down as your score.

Rating	Age—	10	11	12	13	14	15	16	17
						Feet			
Excellent		138	151	165	185	208	221	238	249
Presidential Award		122	136	150	175	187	204	213	226
Good		118	129	145	168	181	198	207	218
Satisfactory		102	115	129	147	165	180	189	198
Poor		91	105	115	131	146	165	172	180

Key: The throw for distance is measured in *feet* from the takeoff line to the spot where the object lands first. The numbers on the chart show the number of feet the ball should travel for each age.

Note: If you are under ten years old, use the test as an exercise and *do not try* to see if you can keep up with older boys and girls.

THROW FOR DISTANCE (GIRLS)

Rating	Age—	10	11	12	13	14	15	16	17
						Feet			
Excellent		84	95	103	111	114	120	123	120
Presidential Award		71	81	90	94	100	105	104	102
Good		69	77	85	90	95	100	98	98
Satisfactory		54	64	70	75	80	84	81	82
Poor		46	55	59	65	70	73	71	71

The Basketball Throw

To make a good basketball throw, you must start by holding the basketball with two hands before releasing it with just one hand. Basketballs are too large for youngsters to control with one hand. So try this event with a junior-size basketball instead of the larger regulation size.

The grip for the basketball throw must be studied very carefully. Rest the basketball in the palm of your throwing hand. Spread your fingers around and under the ball. Bend your wrist so that the basketball also rests against the lower end of the forearm. Press your fingers slightly upward against the ball. Now place your other free hand on the top inside portion of the ball for better control. You are, in fact, carrying the ball with two hands—until the actual one-hand throw is made.

MAKING THE THROW. To make the throw on the run, take a position about six to twelve feet behind the throwing (foul) line. Start your run with both hands carrying the ball off the hip of your throwing side. The weight of your body is on the back foot. As you make the last step or hop, shift your throwing arm back and to your throwing side. Slowly remove your free hand from the ball. Quickly shift your weight to the front foot. Remember to keep the basketball from "slipping" out of your hand by holding it with your fingers, the palm of your hand, and lower end of your forearm. At the same time, the throwing arm starts an overhead throwing motion. Release the ball with your body behind the throw, and follow through by bringing the rear foot forward.

Practice this throw with a partner. See who makes the best throw out of three.

Hints

1. Make sure you find a safe area for all the throwing events before you practice.

2. Concentrate on the baseball, basketball, and light shot-put skills.

3. Practice the javelin, discus, and shot-put only with an adult or teacher available.

4. Do warm-up exercises before you go "all-out" in the throwing events.

Drills and Exercises

It takes powerful fingers, wrists, arms, and shoulders to throw an object for distance. Here are some exercises for you.

ARM AND WRIST DEVELOPERS. Shorten a broomstick to a length of one foot. Drill a hole at the center. Tie a two- to five-pound weight with strong cord through the hole so the weight hangs about three feet below the rod.

Grasp the rod with both hands, raise the arms to shoulder height, and roll and unroll the weight. Many sports champions carry one of these wrist developers in their traveling bags wherever they go.

GRIP AND WRIST DEVELOPER. Keep a sponge ball in your pocket so that at any moment you can take the ball out of your pocket and squeeze it, first in one hand and then the other, 100 times. Put the ball back in your pocket, and then an hour later do 100 more squeezes in each hand. Do this exercise several times a day, and in a matter of weeks you will have a powerful grip.

THROWS WITH BUNDLE OF MAGAZINES. Tie together a bundle of old magazines, weighing five to eight pounds. Rest the bundle on your hand as if it were a *shot-put*. Now see how far you can "put" (push) the bundle of magazines.

Tie together magazines that measure about a total of one inch in thickness. (Maybe you have an old mail-order catalogue to use.) Take a *discus thrower's grip* and see how far you can "hurl" this discus.

SOCCER BALL THROW. See how far you can throw a soccer ball. Use the same skills as you did for the basketball throw.

BASEBALL AND BASKETBALL SHOT-PUT. Use a softball or basketball and practice the shot-put skills.

BASEBALL AND BASKETBALL SIDE-ARM THROWS. See how far you can "hurl" or throw a baseball and basketball for distance, using a side-arm throw.

10

It's a Girls' Sport, Too!

Yes, track and field is certainly a girls' sport, and it is very popular around the world. Girls are competing in running, jumping, and throwing events in elementary schools, high schools, and colleges. All over the country you can see big girls and little girls trying their skills in the park or playground, or at the YWCA, in the Girl Scouts, and with church groups.

Girls' track and field rules are different from those used by boys, but most of the learning skills are the same.

It was not this way many years ago.

Women not Allowed at Olympic Games

The Ancient Olympic Games in Greece were for men only. The ladies were not even allowed as spectators. Some ladies were caught watching the competitions from treetops or through knotholes in the stadium, and they were captured and punished.

Then, some 2,500 years ago, a brave and popular lady named Hippodameosia, decided to help organize a program for girls' competition. She organized the Heraea Games for women only. Even the spectators were all women. She named the festival in honor of Hera, the wife

GIRLS "GO" FOR 50-YARD DASH
(1900-1918)·

of the great Zeus, a popular Greek god. The competition took place every four years, and it allowed the girls to test their skills in foot-racing events only.

The competitors wore a short tunic—a high-waisted dress—that fell between the knees and hips. It slipped over the left shoulder only, leaving the right shoulder and breast uncovered. The girls were in good condition and ran barefooted, with their hair swinging down over their shoulders.

When the Roman empire conquered Greece, women's track and field competition stopped.

Modern Track and Field Meets Begin

Girls did not take part in the first Modern Olympic Games track and field events in 1896. However, they were allowed as spectators, and as their interest increased, women all over Europe became aware of the Olympic games.

France was the first nation to organize a women's track club to promote competition. Austria soon followed France's lead, and then in 1919 England began to sponsor championship track and field meets. Soon Belgium, Italy, Poland, Germany, Norway, and Switzerland formed women's track and field clubs.

Interest in women's track competition spread to Japan and to South America, and by 1925 to every corner of the globe.

The first International Women's Track and Field Meet was held in Monte Carlo in 1921. Five countries and about 110 women competed. New interest was created, but girls were still not allowed to compete in the regular Olympic track and field events, although they were competing in other Olympic events such as swimming and tennis.

After the International (World) Ladies Games in 1926, it was agreed by the International Amateur Athletic Federation that, starting with the 1928 Olympic games, women were to be allowed to compete in five track and field events. Women held their own World Championship Games again in 1934. After the regular 1936 Olympics, the International Amateur Athletic Federation agreed to allow the girls to compete in more track and field events. In today's Olympics, girls and women compete in the sprints and middle-distance running, hurdles, relays, long jump, high jump, discus, javelin, shot-put, and modern Pentathlon events.

First American Women's Competition

Many historians believe that the first American track and field competition for women began at Vassar College, Poughkeepsie, New York, in 1895. The early meets were at first held only for girls of college age.

Girls' Track and Field Organizations

Women teachers and coaches began to form national organizations that would not only promote track and field meets, but also work to improve the rules of the sport. High schools and elementary schools started to teach track and field skills to all boys and girls. Great interest developed and many organizations began to hold track and field meets for girls.

The Amateur Athletic Union (AAU), now sponsors a Junior Olympic Track and Field Program every year for young boys and girls. City recreation departments and colleges sponsor many meets. Each of these organizations has its own rules and regulations. All are interested in healthy competition for youngsters.

One of the most popular organizations is the Division of Girls' and Women's Sports of the American Association for Health, Physical Education, and Recreation. Today, this organization publishes coaching guides and rule books for many different sports events that are held in elementary schools, high schools, and colleges.

Girls Win World Championships

American girls and women compete in sports events all over the world. They travel everywhere to run, jump, and throw against teams from many different countries. They win world championships, too. But most of all, they are finding out that they can have fun making new friends and learning how to keep healthy.

Official Girls' Events

Official events for championship meets for girls in *grades four to six* are recommended by the Division of Girls' and Women's Sports. The *track events* are the twenty-five-yard and fifty-yard dashes; 100-yard and 200-yard regular relays; 100-yard and 200-yard shuttle relays; fifty-yard hurdle. The field events are baseball, softball, basketball, and soccer throws; and standing and running broad jumps, and running high jump.

The events for girls in *grades seven to nine* are the same as those for grades four to six, with the addition of five events. These additional events are the seventy-five-yard dash, 100-yard regular relay, 300-yard shuttle relay, seventy-yard hurdles, and the eight-pound shot-put.

PASSING THE BATON
Blind Pass

Youngsters *below the fourth grade* also have the opportunity to join the fun. Elementary schools and recreation departments teach the different skills needed to take part in the shorter-distance dashes and relays, as well as in jumping and throwing events. Did you ever try the hop-step-jump? If you were a good "hop-scotch" player, you might be a good jumper, too.

Training for Track and Field

Before a girl competes in her favorite track and field events, she must have permission from her doctor and parents or guardian. Teachers will help with training suggestions for sports.

Girls should read the chapters in this book that concern their favorite track and field events, and learn about the different skills that must be practiced. Then they should write down in a *special track and field notebook* the many hints, drills, and exercises mentioned at the ends of the chapters. To get in good condition, these drills should be seriously worked on.

The women you admire most, whether they are teachers, nurses, actresses, scientists, or champion athletes, are healthy, active, and alert. They are people who prepared and trained themselves well for the jobs they do. Each girl should be a doer. Learn the health rules and skills. Get out of doors and practice with other girls, and have your teachers and parents help whenever possible.

11

Getting Ready for the Big Meet

There are many things that must be attended to before the day of the Big Meet.

Is the competition open to anyone? Are only members of a team allowed to enter the competition? Where is the meet going to be held? What events are offered? Do you have the right equipment? Is there a competent referee, starter, scorer? Do you have a team captain?

These and many more questions must be answered before the track and field meet starts. Of course, it is most important that each boy and girl be physically fit and trained before the day of the meet.

Keeping Fit

Remember always keep yourself healthy and strong.

1. Follow the training rules, hints, and exercises in each chapter.
2. Practice as often as you can at a safe place.
3. Report any soreness or bruises to your parents, guardian, teacher, or doctor. Delay in reporting an injury could be serious.
4. Eat the right kinds and amounts of food.
5. Get the right amount of rest and sleep.

6. Do not neglect your study habits.

7. Keep your body clean.

8. Do not be discouraged if you do not do well. The important thing is that you are active in a healthy sport.

Choosing a Track and Field Area

Where are you going to have the running, jumping, and throwing events? Is it going to be an indoor or an outdoor meet?

You must remember that indoor meets require a school or park gymnasium. Outdoor meets usually require a football field with a running track around it. Most regulation indoor and outdoor track and field areas are not available for younger competitors. Do not let the lack of facilities and equipment stop you from healthy competition.

Find a safe place. If you can use an official field or large gymnasium, fine; if not, look for open spaces in a park, playground, or empty large area. Ask the owners of the empty open area if you can use it for a track and field meet. You must have the owner's permission to use the field. You might send him a letter or have a committee call on him. Ask teachers and coaches if the school gymnasium can be used for an indoor meet.

Now, assuming that you have obtained your place, let's find out how to make an outdoor track and field area. These instructions can also be used, with very few changes, for indoor competition.

How to Make Your Own Track and Field Area

Remove all loose stones. Rake away all loose grass and shrubs.

If your running events are going to be held on grass, cut the grass close to the earth. Make sure the running area is level. Check for sharp holes or bumps in the ground.

Now check for safe areas where the competition in field events will be held. Decide what jumping and throwing events will be safe.

Do you have a high-jump pit? Can you dig one? Can you fill it with sand, wood shavings, or foam rubber?

Is the ground for the shot-put circle, baseball and basketball throws level? Be sure to clear these areas of all loose shrubs and stones.

Use a big roller to level and smooth the ground after you have the track and field areas cleared. Dad might help you with his lawn roller or perhaps you could borrow one.

Check the size of the area you need for the various field events by rereading this book's chapters on each event you are going to include in your big meet.

Have your parents, guardian, or teacher check the area for safety.

If the meet is indoors, use thick mats or foam rubber for the high-jump pit. Check for safety if you plan on having the indoor shot-put event. Some of your track

BOYS SPRINTING

BOYS HURDLING

events will be for a shorter distance than if held outdoors. Throwing events will be limited.

Marking the Track and Field

Mark your running lanes at least three-feet apart.
Older runners use four-foot wide lanes.

Running is always done *counterclockwise*. This
means that instead of running in the direction that the
hands of a clock do, you run in the opposite direction.
The left side of the runner is toward the inside of the
track.

Mark the lanes with whitewash or lime lines by at-
taching one end of a piece of string to a peg or stick
secured to the ground at the starting line and one end
to a peg at the finish line.

Use the same whitewash markings to draw the starting
and finish lines.

You can use the same whitewash to mark the shot-
put circle and the starting line for the throwing events.

GIRLS RELAY

For indoor events, regular chalk or removable tape can be used for your markings.

If you do not have a jumping board for the running broad jump, mark a white line eight inches wide across the runway.

Equipment and Supplies

Here is a list of supplies that may help you when getting ready for a big meet:

1. Rule book.
2. Medical service and first-aid kit.
3. Individual numbers that can be printed on a plain sheet of paper and fastened on the back of the shirt of each contestant.
4. Score book and score cards.
5. Hurdles.
6. Yarn for the finish line of the running events.
7. A whistle, loud caller, or a starter's pistol and blank cartridges for only adults to use.
8. List of young people entered in the different events.

9. List of officials.

10. Stopwatches.

11. Steel or cloth measuring tapes to measure distances for jumping and throwing events.

12. Batons for relay races.

13. Starting blocks and mallets or hammers to secure blocks on the ground.

14. Pencils and pads of paper.

15. Shot-put, baseballs, softballs, basketballs, soccer balls for the throwing events.

16. Rake to level dirt, sand, or sawdust in the jumping landing pit.

17. High-jump standards.

18. Crossbars or yarn for high-jump standards.

19. Ropes and flags to mark off safety areas for throwing events.

Check individual chapters in this book for other suggestions.

There are other items you may wish to have, but this list serves only as a reminder. You can have a track and field meet without all of the items mentioned. Just be certain to safeguard yourself and your friends and competitors.

Your Personal Uniform

Your regular physical education gym uniforms are fine for track and field competition—gym or "boxer" type shorts and T-shirts or blouses. A pair of sneakers and sweat socks will complete the uniform you need to enjoy track and field.

If you do not have gym uniforms, an old pair of dungarees and shirt or sweater will do.

Do not plan to purchase regular spiked track shoes without the advice of your teacher, parents, or guardian.

One way to get sports uniforms and equipment is to buy them yourself. This could be expensive. Some teammates might not be able to afford to buy them.

There are many ways to earn your sports equipment, either by working as a team or by working alone.

WORKING AS A TEAM. Let your parents, guardian, or teachers know that your track and field team is going to form working groups to earn money for uniforms and equipment.

Work on paper drives. Collect old books and have a sale. Give special shows at school, church, or at home. Puppet shows, card tricks or other magician's stunts, playing musical instruments, or a one-act play, or your own favorite show are all good ideas. Be alert for other group work opportunities.

WORKING ALONE. There are many fine jobs you can do alone to earn money. It all depends on where you live. Do you live in the city or the country? Some ideas you may choose are:

1. Deliver newspapers.	9. Pull weeds.
2. Shine shoes.	10. Water lawns.
3. Run errands.	11. Rake leaves.
4. Deliver packages.	12. Walk dogs.
5. Clean the yard.	13. Feed farm animals.
6. Cut grass.	14. Paint or clean
7. Pick fruit or vegetables.	(fences, houses, etc.).
8. Fix old toys.	15. Wash cars.

There are many more. Be careful you don't take a job that is dangerous. Do not let your extra work interfere with your study habits.

Your parents, guardian, or teacher may give you

many more good ideas. Ask them for suggestions before you go into new jobs.

Neighborhood businessmen oftentimes are interested in helping a youngsters' sports club get started.

Young athletes get a real thrill when they know they have earned their own uniforms and equipment.

COMPETING WITHOUT UNIFORMS AND EQUIPMENT. Do not let the lack of regulation uniforms or equipment stop you from taking part in track and field.

Many of our greatest champions got their starts without the best uniforms and equipment when they were young.

Wear old shoes and clothes. Try your favorite run, jump, or throw. As long as the area is safe, have fun. Enjoy the thrill of testing your skill in the different events.

Meet Officials

A large number of officials are needed to run a regulation championship track and field meet.

Unless you get plenty of adult help, start out with as few officials as possible. The main thing is to agree upon what each official's duties are, and then start the competition.

MEET DIRECTOR. This official is responsible for seeing that every detail for the meet is ready. He sees that every official is notified of his duties. *Have the duties and responsibility of each official written on small cards.* The meet director also sees that the field is marked correctly for each event.

TEAM CAPTAIN. Select a team captain. He should be a person who enjoys track and field and also gets along with his teammates. Teammates must have respect for him because he represents them when an argument arises. He discusses points of disagreement and questions or rulings with the meet director or track and field referees, if you have them.

THE COACH OR MANAGER. Should be an older person. He has to decide who will be entered in the different events. He must settle all decisions for the team. If you don't have a coach or manager, the team captain should take over these duties.

CLERK OF COURSE. He has the list of all contestants entered in the different events. He checks their names at the start of each event. Every young athlete is checked for correct uniform and also for the large number worn pinned on the back of his shirt. The clerk of course also tries to keep the events moving according to a time schedule.

FINISH JUDGES. Have three judges assigned to pick a first-, second-, and third-place winner. The first-place judge is selected as the *head judge*. He has a separate card with the names of the contestants for each event. This card is filled out at the end of each event with the names of the three winners and is then taken to the score keeper.

TIMERS. To check the time of each runner, you will select a timer. He will stand near the judges at the finish line and will report the winner's time to the head judge.

STARTER. He starts all races with a whistle or any other instrument that the runners can hear. You may always use the shouted word "go" if you don't have a whistle. *Do not use a starter's gun. Only adults are to use this equipment*. The starter should study the sprinter's starting responsibility in Chapter 3.

SCORERS OR SCORE KEEPERS. Have two to four persons assigned to keep score. One should be designated as the *head scorer*. He is to record the official score of the meet. He lists the names of the winners handed to him by the track judges and the time of the first-place winner. He also records the names, heights, and distances handed to him by the judges of the field events.

FIELD JUDGES. There should be two field judges for each *jumping and throwing event*. One judge should be elected as the *head field judge* for each event. For the throwing events, one judge stands near the starter's throwing or foul line. The second judge stands near the area where the thrown object will land. The two judges must record the distance on the score card with the three winners' names and hand it to the chief scorer. For the broad jump, one judge stands near the takeoff board, while the second judge checks the spot of the landing. The judges for the high jump will take a position at each side of the crossbar.

ANNOUNCER. Try to get a portable loud-speaker. The announcer can keep the contestants and fans alert to what is happening. He has information on all the participants and the events, and can make the entire meet more interesting with his comments and statistical reports.

OTHER HELPERS. Boys and girls who are not able to participate physically should be utilized as additional helpers, to make for a smooth-running meet. Some youngsters cannot take part in track and field because their doctors will not allow them. Maybe they would still like to be part of the team by being a helper. You need:

1. Two persons to hold the yarn at the finish line for the running events.

2. Two or more persons to act as messengers for the judges, timers, clerk of course, or announcer.

3. Two or more to be in charge of the track and field equipment.

4. One or more helpers to rake and level the jumping pit after each jump and to replace the crossbar for the high jump.

5. Four or more to help set up and remove the hurdles.

6. Two each to help retrieve the baseballs, basketballs, and soccer balls after each throw—six helpers in all.

7. Two or more to write and publish a story about the highlights of the meet for the school or local newspapers.

This indicates that it takes a lot of people to run a track and field meet. Quite true for a large meet, but do not let this stop you. You need only yourself and a friend to test your skill in a running, throwing, or jumping event. If you can get more friends interested, then try to organize a meet as big as you can handle.

Arranging for a Meet

The coach, captain, boy or girl selected as team secretary makes the arrangements for a meet. The person assigned to this duty can arrange for a meet against another team by phone, letter, or in person.

You must see that the other team coach or captain is contacted days in advance of the date set for the meet.

A written record should be kept to show where the meet will be held, what events will be offered, and what rules will be used. Also to show who will supply the equipment, and to come to an agreement on a scoring system.

Your Rules for Track and Field

Boys and girls, young and old, enjoy the sports of track and field. The rules for your competition will not be the same as those for older boys and girls. However, the skills you learn and practice are the very same. That is the most important thing for now.

Your teacher, parent, or doctor will let you know when you are ready to compete within the rules followed by older athletes.

Read the different chapters in this book and learn about the different rules for each event. Then use the rules that are suggested for young people your age.

Number of Events You Enter

The number of events a youngster is allowed to enter in one meet depends upon the rules agreed upon by the meet directors or team captains.

First, you must be certain that you are in condition to participate well in one event before you try to compete in more than one.

It is considered a good idea to allow young boys and girls the opportunity to compete in the two or three events in which they are best qualified. Usually the three events should be limited to one field and two track events, or two field events and one track event.

Length of the Big Meet

The length of your meet will depend on:

1. The number of different events on the program.
2. Number of youngsters entered in the meet.
3. Number of officials and helpers working at the meet.
4. Location and condition of the track and field you will use.
5. Supplies and equipment you plan to use.

You learned earlier in the book that some championship meets last several days. Others can start and finish in one hour or less. You could plan to sponsor a meet made up of different kinds of relay races only. As a first try it is always a good idea to limit your program of events so you can finish the meet in about one hour. After you have more experience, you may wish to increase the length of the meet by increasing the number of events and entries.

Do not let the lack of equipment or fields stop you from competing. Have fun! Compete—even if you and a few friends set up just a few sprint races to see who is the fastest, or throw the baseball for distance, or try the broad jump and hop-step-jump.

Get into the action! Before you know it, others will want to join in on the fun.

12

Scores and Records

Did you know that every member of a track and field meet receives a report card? After every meet the coaches and athletes study it to see where and how the competitors can improve. Where does the material for the report come from? Who determines the runners', or throwers', or jumpers' grades? What kind of records are kept for each athlete? For each team?

It all begins on the track or field during the day of competition. This is when the head finish judges declare a winner for each event. But not many fans see the tremendous amount of material that is collected by other people who help to prepare the whole report.

Head Score Keeper

There is a head score keeper for each track and field meet. He usually is not a member of either team. He is often hired by the conference or organization, with the agreement of each participating team.

The score keeper must know the rules of the sport and he must be accurate with figures. He has gathered a great deal of material telling him about the teams and athletes entered in the meet.

The score keeper and his assistants are usually located in a section high in the stands called the "press box." The sports writers and the radio and TV announcers are also located in the press box. These men and women can see the entire track and field area.

Many of the questions the head score keeper must answer and report on will come from the head finish judges of each event. All the facts about the competitors in each event are listed on the head finish judges' sheets. After each event, this information is directed to the head score keeper by messenger or by two-way phone.

The official head scorer must know what *scoring system* will be used for the meet. He learns something about each participant from the information given on the team's entry forms. He must have the *official program* showing the time each event will start, the participants' names, numbers, event entered, ages, weights, heights, towns, schools, and past records in each of the events. But most important, he must have ready a *master meet scoring record sheet*.

Team Records

These are some of the more important team matters the head score keeper will report on during the meet competition:

1. Name of the winning team.
2. Name and score of each team entered.
3. Name of events won and lost by each team.
4. How well the team performed in the running events.
5. How well the teams performed in the relay-race events.

6. How well the teams performed in the jumping events.

7. How well the teams performed in the throwing events.

8. How well the teams performed in the hurdle events.

9. Length of the meet (days or hours).

10. Wind velocity (miles-per-hour wind).

11. Weather conditions (rain, cold, hot, etc.).

12. Kind of turf used (artificial, grass, cinders).

13. Condition of competitors' equipment.

14. Condition of the field equipment.

15. Number of team and individual penalties, if any.

Player Records

These are some of the more important matters the head score keeper will report on for each competitor:

1. The name and events entered by each member of the team.

2. The number of points he scored in the meet.

3. The record time he ran a race.

4. The record distance he made in the jumping or throwing events.

5. Who ran the short sprints best?

6. Who ran the longer-distance runs best?

7. Did the members of the relay team show good teamwork?

8. Did the competitor use the correct form or skills in the run, jump, or throw?

9. Was he injured during the meet competition?

10. Did he show skill in passing a runner?

11. Did he argue with the officials?

12. Did he break a school, club, college, or world record?

At the conclusion of the meet, the head score keeper gives a report to the coaches or managers of the teams. He also sends a copy of the report to the commissioner or secretary of the conference or organization sponsoring the track and field meet. If a world record is broken, the report must be sent to the International Amateur Athletic Federation. All these records are kept by each organization as an account of the history of track and field.

Coach and Athlete Study the Records

Did you know that each official track and field team has its own office for keeping these records? This helps the coach to study the strong and weak points of each team member. These records are also posted on the bulletin board of the team's dressing room so everyone may study them. The athletes are graded on their performance ability. The records also help to guide coaches on how best to concentrate their time during practice periods.

Now you can see why these records are so important. This is why you should start keeping your own record book. It will help you improve as you continue to know more about yourself and your opponents.

Track and Field "Program"

Before a track and field meet, many fans buy programs. They contain a number of pages similar to a magazine and provide a lot of information. Much of this information is taken from the entry-blank forms mailed to the meet director. These programs give the names of the athletes and the teams they represent. They list the team rosters and note the names of individual and meet record holders. Often the programs include blank spaces for the fans to write in the names and records of the persons winning the different events.

Many times this information is also printed in the daily newspapers a day or two before the competition.

There are different systems used for scoring in track and field. Here is one of the most popular. A meet committee usually decides on the scoring system to be used.

SCORING FOR RUNNING, THROWING, JUMPING EVENTS (NO RELAYS)

Number of Places to Select	Points Given for Scoring First to Sixth Place					
	1st place	2nd place	3rd place	4th place	5th place	6th place
2	5	2	0	0	0	0
3	5	3	1	0	0	0
4	5	3	2	1	0	0
5	6	4	3	2	1	0
6	10	8	6	4	2	1

The number in the far left column usually represents the number of teams entered in the event. For example: two places only are selected when two teams are entered; three places when three teams are entered; four places when four teams are entered; five places when five teams are entered; and six places when six teams or more are entered.

Scoring for relay races is different from the scoring system used in all other events.

Number of teams entered	Points Given for Scoring First to Fifth Place				
	1st place	2nd place	3rd place	4th place	5th place
2	5	0	0	0	0
3	5	3	0	0	0
4	5	3	2	0	0
5	6	4	3	2	0
6	10	8	6	4	2

The columns listed for scoring the different relay races are similar to those used for the running, jumping, and throwing events. The only big difference is that no points are scored for a sixth-place finish.

SAMPLE SCORE SHEET FOR TRACK EVENTS
(Separate Sheet for Each Event)

Age 10–11 Finals			50-yard Dash (Pick First Six Place Winners)			
Name	No.	School	Lane Position	Time	Place	Points
Bobby	6	Owls	1	7.3	6	1
Danny	4	Eagles	2	7.1	4	4
Art	12	Badgers	3	7.5	8	0
Allen	3	Beavers	4	7.0	3	6
Charles	11	Giants	5	6.9	2	8
Jim	9	Bears	6	6.8	1	10
Ron	2	Lions	7	7.2	5	2
Eddie	7	Colts	8	7.4	7	0

This sample score sheet shows that eight youngsters ran in the fifty-yard dash finals for the ten-to-eleven-year age group. Only the first six runners crossing the finish line score points for this race. The points earned are added toward the team total at the end of the meet competition. The *running time* is measured in seconds and tenths of seconds. The sample score sheet shows that the number-one-place winner ran the dash in six and eight-tenths seconds. The "*No.*" column shows the number that is pinned on the back of the shirt of the runner.

SAMPLE SCORE SHEET FOR FIELD EVENTS
(Separate Sheet for Each Event)

Age 10-11		Finals	Standing Broad Jump (Pick First Six Place Winners)					
			Final Trials					
			1	*2*	*3*	*Best*		
Name	*No.*	*School*	*Ft.In.*	*Ft.In.*	*Ft.In.*	*Effort*	*Place*	*Points*
Don	2	Panthers	6–4	6–2	6–2	6–4	5	2
Ronny	12	Wildcats	6–1	6–2	6–0	6–2	6	1
Jerry	4	Horsemen	6–8	6–7	6–9	6–9	3	6
Len	6	Warriors	6–0	6–1	6–1	6–1	7	0
Burl	3	Vikings	6–6	6–5	6–6	6–6	4	4
Johnny	8	Troopers	7–1	6–8	7–0	7–1	1	10
Chuck	11	Trojans	5–11	5–11	5–10	5–11	8	0
Stan	9	Bisons	6–10	6–11	6–10	6–11	2	8

This sample score sheet shows that eight youngsters competed in the standing-broad-jump finals for the ten-to-eleven-year age group. Only the first six jumpers going the farthest distance score points for this event. Points earned are added toward the team total at the end of the meet. The jumping distance is measured in feet and inches. Each jumper repeats the exercise three times. The *best effort* or jump is measured for the final score.

For example: The first number shows the feet, and the second number shows the inches. Johnny broad jumped for the greatest distance. His 7–1 means he jumped seven feet and one inch to win the event.

The score sheets should carry the following information: (a) name of meet, (b) date of meet, (c) signatures of head judge, timer, score keeper, and director of the meet.

EXPLANATION OF THE TEAM FINAL SCORE SHEET.

—Eight teams entered the two-day championship meet.

—Hawks runner wins twenty-five-yard dash. Receives ten points.

—Cardinals get one point for sixth place in twenty-five-yard dash.

—Packers, Browns get no points for twenty-five-yard dash.

—Hawks get ten points for first place in 100-yard regular relay.

—Tigers get two points for fifth place in 100-yard regular relay.

—Raiders, Cardinals, Rams get no points for 100-yard regular relay.

—You get the total score by adding all points listed for each team.

—Hawks won first place (championship) with seventy-five points.

Newspaper Reports

Your local newspaper prints a record of all track and field meets during the outdoor and indoor seasons. One popular report is known as "Meet Results," which tells what happened between the teams competing. Two other reports are known as "Time Schedule of Events" and "Meet Forecast." The fans watch for this information.

SAMPLE TEAM FINAL SCORE SHEET

(Two-day Championship Meet   Age 10-11-year Group)

Teams	25-yard dash	50-yard dash	100-yard dash	100-yard regular relay	200-yard regular relay	25-yard shuttle relay	50-yard shuttle relay	200-yard medley relay	Softball throw	Basketball throw	Shot-put (light)	Standing broad jump	Running broad jump	Hop-step-jump	High jump	Tug-of-war	Total score	Place winners
Falcons	4	10	10	4		10	6	6	1		2	4			6		59	6th
Raiders	2	1	1	2	2	6	2	1	10	6	8	4	6	1	8	10	46	8th
Hawks	10	2	4	10		4	10	8		1	1	1		8	10	4	75	1st
Cardinals	1	8	6		10	8	8	2	8			1	1	10			62	4th
Tigers	8	1	8	2		4	8	10	6	8	10	6	10	10	4	1	66	3rd
Packers		6	8	8	6	8	4			2	6	2	10	2	8	8	68	2nd
Rams	6		2	8	4	8		4		10	6	8	4	6	2	2	60	5th
Browns		4	2	6	8	2			2	4	4	10	2	4	1	6	55	7th

Scoring System: *Five* places for relays—10, 8, 6, 4, 2. Six places for other events—10, 8, 6, 4, 2, 1.

SIGNATURE HEAD SCORE KEEPER:

NAME OF MEET: PLACE OF MEET:

SIGNATURE HEAD SCORE KEEPER: DATE OF MEET:

SAMPLE "MEET RESULTS" REPORT

HIGH SCHOOL

Two-mile relay: 1, Cardinals (Curt, Mark, Sam, Tom); 2, Cubs; 3, Rovers; 4, Raiders; 5, Robins.   8:20.7

300-yard run: 1, Burl, Stars; 2, Herb, Ghosts; 3, Jimmy, Pioneers; 4, Wally, Tigers; 5, Tom, Troopers; 6, Fred, Colts.   0:34.1

600-yard run: 1, Tony, Colts; 2, Ken, Browns; 3, Lee, Bears; 4, Nick, Eagles; 5, Al, Lions. 1:17.6

Two-mile: 1, Gene, Rams; 2, Stan, Hawks; 3, Vic, Badgers; 4, Joe, Beavers; 5, Merril, Giants.   9:37.6

Pole Vault: 1, Jack, Panthers; 2, Tim, Wildcats; 3, Art, Stars; 4, Mike, Horsemen; 5, Tom, Bisons.   12-9

50 High Hurdles: 1, Hugh, Owls; 2, Edwin, Warriors; 3, Dick, Vikings; 4, John, Trojans; 5, Burt, Falcons. 0:06.3

50-yard run: 1, Herb, Cubs; 2, Frank, Dolphins; 3, Wally, Rangers; 4, Wally, Stellars; 5, Larry, Patriots.   0:05.5

(No team-score totals. Only individual champions declared.)

YOUNG BOYS

50-yard run (13-14): 1, Gary, Packers; 2, Dave, Owls; 3, Burl, Eagles; 4, Steve, Badgers.   0:06.0

50-yard run (11-12): 1, Harvey, Beavers; 2, Frank, Giants; 3, Steve, Bears. 0:06.7

588-yard relay (13-14): 1, Lions (Chuck, Johnny, Burl, Len); 2, Colts; 3, Panthers. 1:13.5

294-yard relay (11-12): 1, Wildcats (Len, Jerry, Ronny, Don); 2, Horsemen; 3, Warriors.   0:40.3

294-yard relay (10 and under): 1, Vikings (Wayne, Rafael, Walt, Dominic); 2, Troopers; 3, Trojans. 0:42.7

294-yard run (13-14): 1, Chris, Falcons; 2, Willis, Ghosts; 3, Willie, Bisons. 0:38.7

Team Scoring—Packers, 24; Owls, 16; Eagles, 12; Lions, 6; Badgers, 3; Beavers, 2; Panthers, Vikings, Warriors, Troopers, Ghosts, Bisons, 1 each.

50-yard run (13-14): 1, Criss, Blues; 2, Elisa, Oranges; 3, Pat, Blacks.   0:07.0

50-yard run (11-12): 1, Amy, Whites; 2, Jene, Greens; 3, Ruth, Browns.   0:07.2

294-yard relay (13-14): 1, Yellows (Celia, Betty, Josie, Olga); 2, Reds; 3, Violets. 0:41.2

294-yard relay (11-12): 1, Lilacs (Frances, Ella, Donna, Ann); 2, Roses; 3, Tulips. 0:43.5

294-yard relay (10 and under): 1, Peaches (Sue, Vi, Cindy, Mary); 2, Daffodils; 3, Blues.   0:47.4

Team Scoring—Blues, 13; Peaches, 7; Blacks and Greens, 6 each; Whites and Lilacs, 5 each; Oranges and Roses, 4 each; Daffodils and Reds, 3 each; Browns, Violets, Tulips, 1 each.

EXPLANATION OF REPORT.

—High-school two-mile relay won by Cardinals team made up of Curt, Mark, Sam, Tom. The Robins team came in fifth. Winners' time was eight minutes, twenty and seven-tenths seconds.

—High-school 300-yard run shows Burl from the Stars team won in thirty-four and one-tenth seconds.

—Pole vault was won by Jack from the Panthers in twelve feet, nine inches.

—The numbers—(13-14), (11-12), (10 and under) —listed after each event for young boys and girls means the age group of the runners.

—The team scoring shows the Packers won the young boys' competition with twenty-four points. As for the young girls, the Blue team won with thirteen points.

SAMPLE TIME SCHEDULE OF EVENTS

Finals

11:00 A.M.—shot-put
1:00 P.M.—pole vault
      hop-step-jump
      high-hurdle relay
2:00 P.M.—440 relay
2:15 P.M.—440 hurdles
2:25 P.M.—440-yard run
2:35 P.M.—mile run
2:45 P.M.—100-yard run
2:55 P.M.—steeplechase
3:20 P.M.—120 high hurdles
3:30 P.M.—220-yard semi-finals
3:40 P.M.—880-yard run
3:50 P.M.—3-mile run
4:10 P.M.—120 high hurdles
4:15 P.M.—220-yard finals
4:25 P.M.—mile relay

CONFERENCE MEET FORECAST

Conference Record	Best Performer of Year	Best Record
100—(9.4)	Bob, Owls	9.4
200—(20.6)	Paul, Eagles; Bill, Badgers;	
	Henry, Beavers	21.2
440—(45.5)	Phil, Giants	47.3
880—(1:47.4)	Danny, Bears	1:48.6
Mile—(3:56.8)	Art, Lions	4:00.4
3-Mile—(13:32.6)	Allen, Colts	13:26.6*
6-Mile—(28:23.8)	Charles, Panthers	28:50.0
120 HH—(13.5)	Jim, Wildcats	13.7
440 IH—(50.4)	Ron, Horsemen	50.4
Steeplechase—(8:46.1)	Rafael, Warriors	8:35.0*
440 Relay—(40.9)	Vikings and Troopers	41.2
Mile Relay—(3:09.1)	Trojans	3:12.1

High Jump—(7-1½)	Willie, Bisons	7.2*
Long Jump—(25-9¾)	Willis, Rovers	26-7½*
Pole Vault—(16-4)	Gary, Robins	16-9¼*
Triple Jump—(51-4¾)	Steve, Falcons	50-10½
Shot-put—(62-1¾)	Vic, Pioneers	59-6½
Discus—(187-2)	Tim, Raiders	187-7
Javelin—(251-5)	John, Hawks	255-2*
Hammer—(208-8½)	Ed, Cardinals	213-9*

An asterisk (*) after figures under *Best Record* column means the athlete's best performance of the year has already broken the former conference record for that event. HH under *Conference Record* column means 120-yard high hurdles. IH means 440-yard intermediate hurdles. The fans will be waiting with excitement to see if the performers can break the record again at this year's regular Conference Championship Meet.

More Records

At the end of every indoor and outdoor season, newspapers and magazines report on the outstanding track and field records. Some of these stories tell about:

1. Best young boys' and girls' records.
2. Best high-school records.
3. Best Conference and Club records.
4. Best college records.
5. New national, world, Olympic records.
6. Best teams of the year.

Sports fans everywhere read these stories. They study them and try to predict next year's championships. Much of this information becomes a lasting record of track and field history.

You, too, should begin to keep your own records. Start your own track and field notebook. Use your skills in arithmetic by keeping a record of your best run, jump, or throw. Add the total number of points you or your favorite star have scored during the season. Work on percentages if you wish to know your personal won-and-lost record for the year. Good record keeping will give you a chance to study your strong and weak points. This is what the champions do.

13

Walking, Jogging, Hiking
—A Family Sport

From the time a child is born, parents wonder when the baby will take his first steps. As the child develops and begins to walk, he becomes aware that by simply moving his legs in a certain manner he can move about in play. As a child grows older, he wants to be on his feet longer and wants to play for longer periods of time. This means that he must have good leg and body muscles, as well as a healthy heart and breathing system.

American Settlers on Foot

How many times have you seen pictures of the early American pioneers walking beside their wagons as they traveled westward, opening up our great country to civilization. Horses pulled the wagons, but in the main, the men, women, and children walked. They had what is known as body "stamina," "staying power," or "endurance."

Less Use of Legs, Less Fitness and Sports

As new ways of travel were discovered, man began to use his legs less and less. Naturally his breathing and muscle systems were also used less and less.

Man soon discovered that in an emergency he needed additional stamina to perform better. He found that regular periods of exercise to build up the stamina of leg and heart muscles made him feel more alert and healthy. And, of course, it helped him enjoy the extra thrills of taking part in sports.

Now let's find out about *walking, jogging, and hiking*.

What Is Walking?

Walking is moving or advancing on foot by your own steps, without running or lifting one foot entirely before the other touches the ground. The walk can be slow or fast, and it is *not* done for competition.

COMPETITIVE WALKING. This is an event that is included in a track and field meet. It is mostly seen in the American and Olympic championship meets. The event is also known as the "heel-and-toe" sport. This is because the rules say the *walker's* heel must touch the ground first, and the toe must be the last portion to leave it. The heel of the front foot must touch the ground before the toe of the back foot leaves the ground.

Don't worry about practicing this kind of walk. For enjoyment, stay with regular walking exercise for now. If you are interested in the competitive walk, see your teacher before spending extra time to prepare for this event.

What Is Jogging?

Jogging is slow-paced running, the kind of gait a player uses to circle the bases after hitting the ball over the fence for a home run in baseball. It is a "slow trot," a speed somewhere between a relaxed running and walking movement.

Hiking calls for walking over different kinds of turf (earth) and distances in parks and other open or scenic areas in the country. The hike can be a brisk walk or a long journey taken with evenly measured, persistent footsteps to reach a certain location.

Join a Club

If you, your family, and friends wish to join a club for walking, jogging, or hiking, contact your city recreation or school office.

Many cities are developing special trails for people who wish to take part in these activities. If your school or neighborhood does not have a club, try to form one, or start your own family club.

Before you, members of the family, or friends begin one of these club programs, it is important that each member has a physical examination. This will inform each person of the distance and speed he is allowed to cover without danger to his health.

How to Walk, Jog, Hike

There is no one best way to enjoy these special activities. The walking, jogging, and hiking body action should feel natural to you.

The style will change with different people. It should be remembered that *you are not going after records to see how fast you are walking, jogging, or hiking*. In these activities you are traveling leisurely for pleasure and distance, so your stride style will be different at times.

In *walking* you should keep your knees and ankles limber, with toes pointed straight ahead. Your head and chest are held high, swinging the legs directly forward from the hip joints. Always push your feet off the ground, and swing the shoulders and arms freely.

In *jogging* there are three different stride styles that are used. The one that is the most popular is called the "heel-to-toe" style. With this style, the jogger first lands on the heel of the front foot, with body rocking forward, and then pushes off on the ball of the foot.

The "flat-foot" style jogger places the *entire* bottom of his front foot on the ground. Persons using this style usually feel a sudden jar or shock when the foot hits the surface.

The "ball-to-heel" style jogger lands on the ball of the front foot, quickly touching the heel on the ground before pushing off for the next step.

The *hiker* usually uses the "heel-to-toe" or "step" style.

Your steps will change a little as you go down or up a hill. Your body lean will also change.

Remember, when taking part in these three activities, try to keep your body in an upright position. Relax the neck and shoulder region by swinging your arms forward and backward freely in a rhythmical motion. Make your strides simple, with good upward and forward knee action. Be sure to breathe through both your nose and mouth. You may wish to review Chapter 4, *Distance Running and Endurance Events,* for more information.

Personal Clothing

No special clothing is necessary to enjoy the benefits of walking, jogging, or hiking. Many stores sell colorful-looking sweat suits, warm-up outfits, and special shoes if you wish to buy them. They have them in sizes for the entire family.

All you really need is old clothing that fits loosely

enough to allow freedom of movement. Dress lightly for warm weather, and wear warm clothing for colder weather. A cap, ear protectors, and gloves are also useful for cold weather.

Socks should be soft, thick, and should fit properly. Cotton or wool sweat socks are suggested. The shoes should be well cushioned and should fit properly. The shoes should have a sole—without heels—that prevents slipping and bends easily. Built-in arch supports are a good idea *if* your doctor recommends them.

Why Walk, Jog, Hike?

There are many good reasons for walking, jogging, or hiking. The President's Council on Physical Fitness and Sports recommends these activities for improving a person's heart, lungs, blood vessels, and muscular strength and endurance. Other reasons are:

—Most everyone can walk, jog, and hike.
—It is cheap, easy, simple, and can be fun.
—It is easy to take part at your own level of physical ability.
—Little equipment is needed.
—It can be done alone, with the family, or friends.
—Helps to improve posture.
—Gets people outdoors.
—Helps to get rid of that tired, dull feeling.
—Helps to take off, and keep off, weight.
—It is a good way to keep in condition for your favorite sport.
—Helps you to feel better, look better, and perform your daily work better.

Did you know that many prisoners of war living in

small cells, cramped for space, jogged and "ran-in-place" to keep fit and stay alive?

How Much Walking, Jogging, Hiking?

There is no one best answer that tells you the distance and speed you should cover in walking, jogging, or hiking.

The best way to find out early is to have your family doctor help you. Another way is to remember how you felt after a long walk, jog, or hike. Did you tire easily? Were your legs sore the next day? Did you feel relaxed during your exercise? The answers to these questions will tell you what distance and at what speed you should practice and enjoy these activities.

One good test to measure your endurance for these activities is listed in Chapter 4. Remember how you scored? Plan your walking, jogging, and hiking according to the rating you received.

Try to follow a regular schedule of walking and jogging. If you can't find a real track, try the park, playground, back yard, or an open field. An indoor gymnasium or even inside your home is also fine. Running-in-place is always good.

The President's Council on Physical Fitness and Sports has written special books that tell adults and older people how much they should take part in these activities.

Walking and Jogging for Life

Walking and Jogging for Life is the "slogan" that many people over the world are talking about. In a way it means that man must use his legs more often if he wishes to stay healthy for a longer time.

Let's see how many more "idea" walks, jogs, or hikes there are. Do any of these three activities:

—With your pal.
—With your dog.

—With your family.
—To do errands.
—To explore nature.
—To explore historic scenes.
—For the fun of it.
—With a camera.
—With a portable radio.

Here are some more ways to get you on your feet:

—Help children and older people who are in wheel-chairs and can't walk. Help them by pushing the wheelchair.
—Walk or jog with the blind. Be their eyes!
—Help people who can't help themselves by collecting money for medical research. Join official groups in a "walkathon" to raise money for the different health organizations and the sick. In a walkathon youngsters and adults are pledged a specific amount by a donor for each mile covered.

You must remember that all these activities have to be fun for you. Do not make them competitive by seeing who can cover the greatest distance. Take part in these activities to help yourself stay in condition. If you like both fun and competition, then you must spend some time learning the skills of your favorite track and field event as set forth in other parts of this book.

14
Everyone Can Enjoy
Track and Field

Glenn Cunningham, the great runner, had polio when he was young. The doctor would not allow him to engage in track and field because of his disability. But he read books, talked to great runners and coaches, and worked hard to strengthen his legs, heart, and breathing. Day after day, week after week, during winter and summer he trained. He worked endlessly, tirelessly, and, eventually, he won several races. Later on, as a young college athlete, he won the world's record in the mile run. He also represented America in the Olympic Games.

Many outstanding men and women could not compete in track and field, and for a number of different reasons. This did not stop them from enjoying the sport.

If you are not able to compete in sports events, you can be active in other ways. Be a member of the team by being the manager or doing some other job for the team.

Check with your parents and your doctor about these suggestions:

SERVE ON THE MEET COMMITTEE. Help arrange for track and field meets. Find the right teams to compete against.

BE AN ASSISTANT SCORE KEEPER. Help the chief score keeper with the scores and records of your team.

BE A REPORTER. Help with the publicity for your team. Make posters and signs to advertise when and where your team will compete, and report the games to the school and neighborhood newspapers.

FOLLOW THE ACTION. Follow the track and field action on TV or radio. Read the magazine and newspaper accounts of the meet highlights. Go to live meets.

HELP THE MEET OFFICIALS. Help assist the meet director, clerk of course, or announcer.

HELP ARRANGE FOR EQUIPMENT AND SUPPLIES. List the condition of the track and field area. Arrange for the equipment and supplies your team will need for the meet. Help mark the track and field.

HELP YOUR TEAM PRACTICE.
1. Check the runners on quick-starting drills, with you acting as the starter.
2. Act as a timer to see how fast a runner covers different distances.
3. Pass the baton to a runner from a standing-still position. Work on the blind and visual passes.
4. Help hold one end of the tape to measure the distance of the broad jump, hop-step-jump, or throwing events.

BE A COACH'S ASSISTANT. Help fill in the names of the team members on an entry blank. Print the training rules on an office machine so each member will have a copy, and print an up-to-date record about each team member.

Wheelchair Track and Field

Thousands of disabled youngsters and adults are competing in competitive track and field events. After World

War II, programs were designed especially for those needing a wheelchair to move about.

A National Wheelchair Athletic Association was organized to establish rules for all wheelchair sports (except basketball) in America. Basketball is controlled by the National Wheelchair Basketball Association.

Track and Field for the Mentally Slow

Another popular organization that promotes sports for the disabled or retarded is the Joseph P. Kennedy, Jr., Foundation. This foundation, which is named for the brother of former President John F. Kennedy, also develops programs for those who are retarded and mentally slow.

Mentally Slow "Champ" Award

The Joseph P. Kennedy, Jr., Foundation sponsors special *fitness* and *champ* award programs. Some of the track and field events included in the champ-award program are the shuttle run, standing broad jump, fifty-yard dash, softball throw, and the 300-yard run and 300-yard walk events. The two other events in the program are sit-ups in one minute and the flexed (bent) arm hang over on the chinning (horizontal) bar.

Find out about these special programs for the physically and mentally handicapped. Ask your teacher or doctor about them.

CHAMPIONSHIP COMPETITION. The organizations named above offer competition to determine:

—Championships for your own neighborhood or school.
—Championships for your state.
—United States Championships.

—World Olympic Championships against other countries.

SPECIAL TRACK AND FIELD EVENTS. Depending on your age, some of the events included in these special meets are:

Throwing for Distance

1. Hard ball or softball
2. Basketball
3. Beanbags
4. Shot-put (lightweight)
5. Javelin (older men, women)
6. Football
7. Soccer ball
8. Discus (a type of ring-toss)

Speed Events

1. There are special speed distances designed for youngsters. Begin with twenty-five-yard distance.
2. Special speed distances for older men and women go up to 220 yards.
3. Shuttle relay races are offered with shorter distances for youngsters and longer distances for older competitors.

Handicapped Athlete of the Year

Each year a *Handicapped Athlete of the Year* award is given to the person who has performed with superior skill and dedication.

Wheelchair Sports Hall of Fame

A permanent record is kept of persons elected to the *Wheelchair Sports Hall of Fame*. These people are honored for their outstanding performance or contribution to wheelchair-sports programs.

Before you choose to help your team, be sure to get the permission of your parents and doctor. If you plan to compete in special-event drills, see that your teacher checks with your parents and family doctor.

Do not be discouraged if you cannot take part in these activities. Keep up with the action by watching the track and field programs on TV, or listen to the sport over the radio. You can also enjoy reading about the sport in your newspapers and in your favorite magazines.

Try to watch track and field meets in person. It's fun to talk about your favorite runner, thrower, or jumper. You are still a loyal fan even if you cannot be active with the team.

If you study track and field and show real knowledge of the various events, you might qualify as a sports announcer for your local radio or TV station.

One day, many years ago, a young athlete was in a terrible automobile accident. The doctor had to amputate his left leg to save the young athlete's life. After the operation, the athlete learned to walk again with the aid of an artificial limb. He never gave up, and he used his knowledge of sports to get a job as a sports announcer. And within a few years he became one of America's best-known sportscasters. His name—Bill Stern.

15

Move Your Feet!
Throw! Jump!

Another great outdoor track and field season has ended. New records were made. New champions were honored. Fans over the world followed the action of their favorite teams, watching:

Runners going for record speeds!
Jumpers soaring in space for more height and distance!
Throwers propelling or exploding objects out of sight!

Because track and field enjoys great worldwide interest, fans can follow their favorites in action the year around. There is an indoor and outdoor season, with track and field meets going on somewhere in the world all year. More and more athletes are taking part. New fans see the action in person. Many more watch it on TV, listen to it on radio, and read the reports in newspapers and magazines.

All over the country you can see open spaces and gymnasiums being used for running, throwing, and jumping events as young boys and girls try out their skills.

Whether you are taking part in real track and field events or simple games, they all demand training, conditioning, coordination, timing, speed, strong heart and breathing system, and an alert mind.

Younger children use and improve early skills in such games as tag, hide-and-seek, "chase," and hopping, jumping, and throwing.

It's healthy! It's fun! It's exciting for everyone!

Get into the action! Move your feet! Throw! Jump!

Glossary

AAU Amateur Athletic Union of America, sponsors of many athletic meets.

Acceleration An even change from a stop or slow rate of speed to a faster rate of speed.

Anchor Leg The fourth or last leg (part) of a four-part relay race.

Anchor Man The fourth or last runner on a relay team.

Blind Pass Made in a relay race when a runner receives the baton without looking back at the baton or the passer.

Breaking Runner leaves the starting line before the official starter's "go" signal or the sound of the pistol shot.

Competitors' Numbers Numbers attached on the backs of each team member for purpose of identification.

Crossbar The bar over which the pole vaulters and high jumpers must go.

Curb The inside edge of the track.

Dead Heat When two or more runners end in a tie by crossing the finish line at the same time.

Decathlon A test made up of ten different track and field events that must be completed by one person to measure his all-around athletic skill.

D.G.W.S. Division for Girls' and Women's Sports of the American Association for Health, Physical Education, and Recreation that promotes athletic events in the United States.

Driving Leg   The leg that gives forward force during the take-off of a race or during the actual running.

Exchange Zone   An area of twenty-two yards marked on the track, where a runner must pass the baton to the next runner in a relay race. (Also known as the passing zone.)

False Start   When a runner leaves the starting line before the signal "go" or sound of pistol.

Finish Posts   Posts installed at each side of the track, to which the finish yarn or tape is attached.

Finish Tape or Yarn   A piece of yarn (tape) stretched across the track directly above the finish line to help the judges decide the winner of the race, the winner being the first runner to hit the yarn or tape.

Free Leg   The leg which is not "pushing off" from the ground. It is "swinging free" ready to hit the ground for the next push-off drive forward.

Gun Up   A warning signal to tell the official judges and timers that the starter's arm is up, ready to signal the start of the race.

Hammer   A throwing event with a sixteen-pound metal ball connected to a single length of steel wire four-feet long attached to a metal handle.

Heat   Preliminary races held to choose the winners who will run in the semi-finals and finals. (Used when there are more runners entered for a race than there are lanes to run all at one time.)

Heraea Games   (1) Known as the first track meet organized for women competitors about 2,500 years ago. (2) The games (or festival) were named in honor of *Hera,* the wife of the great *Zeus,* greatest of the Greek gods.

IAAF   International Amateur Athletic Federation, which approves all World track and field records.

Interscholastic   Competition between schools having grades from seven to twelve.

Jogging   Running at a slow pace or rate of speed.

Landing   The position of the feet and body at the completion (landing) after the pole vault, high jump, broad jump, hop-step-jump, as well as the first-step landing after clearing a hurdle.

Landing Pit   The landing area after completing the pole vault, high jump, broad jump, and hop-step-jump.

Lane   Marked areas between white lines on the track from starting to finish line, where each runner must stay to prevent getting into the path of another runner.

Lap   One complete length of the oval or circular track.

Lead Leg   (1) The first leg (part) of a relay race. (2) First leg to leave the ground for a jump or start of a run.

Lead-off Man   The runner who runs the first leg of a relay race.

Leg   One of the four parts of a relay race; also, part of the body.

Marathon   A contest of long duration, like an extra-inning ball game; also, a track event of extra-long running distance, such as a marathon foot race.

Meters   A unit of measurement, part of the metric system, which is used in most countries of the world. It is used to measure the distances for races in the Olympic games. Examples are: *one meter* is about 39.37 inches—just over one yard; *100 meters* is equal to 328.1 feet or 109 yards, 1.1 feet; *200 meters* is equal to 656.2 feet or 218 yards, 2.2 feet; *800 meters* is equal to 2,624.7 feet or 874 yards, 2.7 feet or almost one-half mile; *1,500 meters* is equal to 1,640 yards, 1.3 feet, and is also known as the *metric mile* because it is closest to the American mile run of 1,760 yards; *2,000 meters* is equal to about 1.24 miles; and *5,000 meters* is equal to about 3.1 miles.

NCAA   National Collegiate Athletic Association that regulates athletic meets among many universities in the United States.

NFSHSAA   National Federation of State High School Athletic Associations that regulates meets among many of the high schools in the United States.

Pace   A rate of moving—for example, setting a slow or fast pace in a long-distance run.

Passer   The runner who passes the baton to the next runner (receiver) in the exchange or passing zone during a relay race.

Passing Zone   An area of twenty-two yards, marked on the track, where a runner must pass the baton to the next runner in a relay race. (Also known as the exchange zone.)

Pentathlon   An activity made up of five different track and field events that must be completed by one person.

Recall   Calling back the runners to get back into the "on your mark" position after a false start was made.

Receiver   The runner who receives the baton from the passer in the passing or exchange zone during a relay race.

Relays (distance)   Also known as *long-distance relays*, as in the four-mile distance race in which each of the four members of a team run one mile.

Relays (make-up)   Races sponsored by different organizations. They might cover distances from one city or town to another, or from one school or park to another.

Relays (middle distance)   Distance runs beyond the sprint distances and shorter than the long-distance relays.

Relays (shuttle "flat")   Races without hurdles, which are run either on the "flat track" or grass portion of the field.

Relays (shuttle hurdle)   Called shuttle because runners race in a "back and forth" direction on the track, with two members lined up on one end of the track facing the other two members of the team at the opposite end.

Relays (sprint)   Shorter-distance runs for each four members of a relay team.

Relays (sprint medley)   Called *medley* because each runner covers a different distance to complete the relay race.

Runway   The running area used just before taking off for a jump or javelin throw.

Scratch Line   The front edge of the takeoff board used in the broad jump, hop-step-jump, and softball and basketball throws.

Steeplechase   A long-distance event that requires the runner to clear twenty-eight to thirty-two hurdles and seven to eight water jumps in order to finish the race.

Straightaway   The straight portion of the track that lies between one curve and the next.

Stride   The distance usually covered by a runner's long step.

Surveyor   A specially trained person who approves the official measurements and markings on the track and field areas.

Takeoff   The action of the body leaving the ground from the spring of the legs in the hurdles, pole vault, high jump, broad jump, and hop-step-jump.

Takeoff Foot   The foot that helps the body drive off the ground in a springlike upward or forward action.

Toe Board or Step Board   Curved four-foot piece of wood on the front of the seven-foot circle used as the foul line for the shot-put.

Triple Jump   Also known as hop-step-jump event.

Visual pass   Made in a relay race when a runner receives the baton by looking back at the passer and the baton.

Index